Integrated Audit Practice Case

SEVENTH EDITION

David S. Kerr + Randal J. Elder + Alvin A. Arens

ARMOND DALTON PUBLISHERS INC.

Armond Dalton Publishers, Inc.
Okemos, Michigan

ISBN 978-0-912503-68-4

Table of Contents
— Assignments Booklet and Permanent File

Guidelines for completing the Integrated Audit Practice Case:

Assignments:

Permanent File:

> **NOTE:** The permanent file is a separate file containing information of a permanent, ongoing nature about the client. The permanent file is normally maintained separate from the current year audit files and is included behind the assignments in this booklet for convenience.

IN ORDER TO SUCCESSFULLY ACCESS THE ELECTRONIC WORKPAPERS, YOU WILL NEED TO CAREFULLY READ AND APPLY THE STEPS BELOW, THEN FOLLOW INSTRUCTIONS IN THE E-MATERIALS PROVIDED ON THE ARMOND DALTON RESOURCES WEBSITE.

- Go to www.armonddaltonresources.com and click on E-Materials.

- Use the E-Materials drop down menu and select Integrated Audit Practice Case, 7th edition.

- Follow the instructions in the E-materials to register on the Armond Dalton Resources website and access the electronic workpapers.

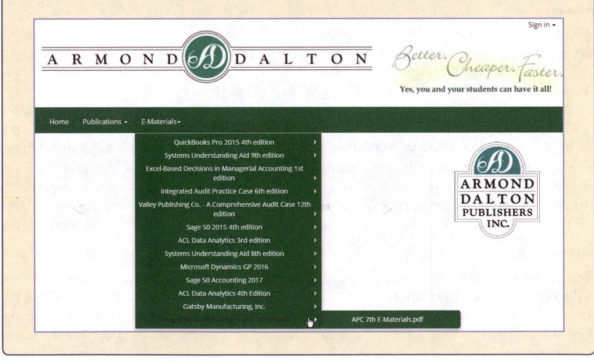

INTRODUCTION: Guidelines for completing the Integrated Audit Practice Case

Overview of the practice case

The *Integrated Audit Practice Case* consists of one booklet containing the assignments and permanent file, a shrink-wrapped set of three-hole punched workpapers, and one folder containing client documents.

(1) Assignments and Permanent File (this booklet)

Assignments

Provides an overview of this practice case and guidance for preparing workpapers, as well as the 10 assignments you will complete in this practice case. The assignments are as follows:

Assignment 1: Review client background information
Assignment 2: Preliminary analytical procedures and risk assessment discussion
Assignment 3: Determine materiality and assess risks
Assignment 4: Assess control risk and plan tests of controls and tests of transactions
Assignment 5: Perform tests of controls and substantive tests of transactions
Assignment 6: Perform audit of accounts receivable
Assignment 7: Perform audit of accounts payable
Assignment 8: Perform audit of cash
Assignment 9: Perform audit of inventory
Assignment 10: Complete the audit

Permanent File

This booklet contains the permanent file workpapers, which provide information about the client's business, industry, and accounting system.

(2) Workpapers

These three-hole punched workpapers are used to complete the assignments and include workpapers used when (1) planning the audit, (2) studying and testing internal controls, including related substantive tests of transactions, (3) performing test of balances, and (4) completing the audit.

Note: We recommend purchasing a 1½-inch, three-ring binder, removing the workpapers from the shrink wrapping, and placing the workpapers in the binder.

> **NOTE:** Many of the workpapers are also provided electronically in Microsoft Excel or Microsoft Word format. See the E-materials at www.armonddaltonresources.com for steps to register on the Armond Dalton Resources website and download the project files.

(3) Client Documents Folder

Contains vouchers, invoices, receiving reports, purchase orders, and other documents you will use to perform many of your audit procedures.

At the beginning of each assignment is a flowchart showing the overall flow of audit procedures and where the assignment fits in that flow. Following the flowchart in each assignment is a discussion of important auditing concepts related to the assignment. The assignment's requirements are then presented; you must perform each of the requirements to complete the assignment. A list of discussion questions concludes each assignment. These discussion questions are optional—your instructor will tell you which questions he or she would like you to answer and whether to turn in hard copies for grading or whether to submit answers online at armonddaltonresources.com.

Learning objectives

The learning objectives for the *Integrated Audit Practice Case* are:

- To help you understand the interrelationships among the audit decisions involved in audit planning, audit testing, and forming the auditor's opinion.
- To obtain hands-on practice in the preparation of an audit workpaper file.
- To develop skills in analyzing transactions and applying auditing knowledge.
- To develop skills in the application of auditing standards.
- To evaluate the audit evidence accumulated to support the auditor's opinion and the issuance of the audit report.

Student's role

You are a first-year member of the audit staff at Lilts Berger & Associates, CPAs. You have been assigned by Charles Ward, the engagement partner, to participate in the audit of Oceanview Marine Company's 2018 financial statements. You will be replacing Bill Cullen, another member of the audit staff at Lilts Berger & Associates, who is working on other audits and does not have the time to complete the audit of Oceanview Marine Company.

Oceanview's year-end is December 31. The current date is February 18, 2019, and you have just replaced Bill. You are to complete the audit and prepare the audit file for Charles Ward's review. This booklet contains the specific assignments you need to perform to complete the audit. The shrink-wrapped material contains the workpapers you will complete during the audit.

Guidelines for preparing audit documentation

Audit workpapers provide the principal source of support for the auditor's opinion. Any document prepared (by the client or auditor) during an audit to support the audit conclusion is considered audit documentation and is appropriately indexed and placed in the audit file. Workpapers are a permanent record of the quality and extent of work performed, including compliance with auditing standards. Proper workpapers constitute the first line of defense in any legal proceeding against an auditor. Therefore, they must be clear, complete, concise, and "speak for themselves."

General guidelines

1. For workpapers completed manually, pencil should be used to facilitate corrections.
2. Be concise, logical, accurate, and complete. Information on each workpaper should be clear to the reader. Workpapers should not contain too much information. Audit tickmark explanations should be complete but also concise.
3. Be neat in preparing workpapers. An auditor's work should be a source of pride, as it will be reviewed several times in the audit process.
4. Initial a workpaper as having been prepared only when the workpaper is completed.

Workpaper information

The preparer should make sure that each workpaper includes the following information:

At the top of each page:
- Client name
- Title describing workpaper contents
- Client's year-end date

In the top-right corner of each page:
- Workpaper index number.
- Initials (either handwritten or typed) of the staff person who completed the workpaper (initial after you have completed all the procedures required for that workpaper).
- Date the workpaper was completed.
- Initials of the senior, manager, and partner who reviewed the workpaper (these will be left blank in the *Integrated Audit Practice Case* because the audit file is yet to be reviewed).

Client involvement

Prior to an audit, the client should be requested to gather the necessary records and (where possible) prepare certain analyses and workpapers. This policy saves time and reduces audit fees. Any workpapers prepared for the auditor by the client should be marked as *"PBC"* (Prepared By Client).

Audit tickmarks

Each CPA firm uses a standard set of audit tickmarks. Standardization facilitates substitution of staff on audit engagements and review of workpapers by seniors, managers, and partners.

The following guidelines should be adhered to:

- Make sure that audit tickmarks are neat and distinguishable.
- Use different tickmarks for different tests.
- Standardize tickmarks within a section as much as possible. For example, in many CPA firms, the capital letter *F* is a standard tickmark used to indicate that a column of numbers has been footed by the auditor. Footed means the numbers have been re-added to verify that the total is correct or that summation formulas have been checked if the schedule is in spreadsheet format.

- In this practice case, all tickmarks used on a specific workpaper should be explained in a "tickmark legend" at the bottom of the workpaper. In the case of a multiple-page document such as the accounts receivable listing, the tickmark legend may appear at the end of that document.
- In the tickmark legend, when explaining tickmarks that refer to another document (for example, "traced to…"), specifically describe which document was used (for example, "traced to cash receipts journal").
- Prepare an explanation for each tickmark only after all work performed for the procedure has been completed.
- Tickmarks are normally placed to the right of a number or text, although the location can vary due to space constraints and the purpose of the tickmark. For example, the *F* usually appears below the column of numbers that has been footed.

Workpaper fonts used in the practice case

Ordinarily, workpapers in an audit file have various types of notes, initials, and signatures In this practice case, initials and signatures are represented by various *hand* and *script* fonts. Audit work performed by Bill Cullen is indicated on the workpapers by the *Times New Roman Italic* font.

When completing workpapers manually, you should <u>use pencil</u> handwriting to conform to common practice. When completing workpapers using the computer, you should use the "Arial" font (to distinguish your work from that of Bill's).

Typical set of audit files

Workpapers are grouped into audit files according to content. The files typically established by auditors for each audit client include:

- Current audit file — Contains all workpapers applicable to the year under audit.
- Permanent file — Contains information of a historical or continuing nature about the audit and the client.
- Corporate tax file (not included in this practice case) — Contains tax returns as filed and/or amended together with notice(s) of assessment or reassessment, notice(s) of objection, and other tax information.

Indexing

Indexing is used to organize the workpapers and to facilitate the cross-referencing and filing of information. Each firm develops a standard method of indexing workpaper files. Your firm, Lilts Berger & Associates, CPAs, uses the following indexing system for current audit files:

Section Number	Description	Location in this practice case
	Audit Planning	
1	Financial Statements	Current Workpapers
2	Analytical Procedures	Current Workpapers
3	Working Trial Balance	Current Workpapers
4	Engagement Letter	Current Workpapers
5	Assessments of Risks and Materiality	Current Workpapers
6	Audit Planning Checklist; Time and Fee Budget	Current Workpapers
	Assess Control Risk; Perform Test of Controls and Substantive Tests of Transactions	
10	Study of Internal Control Environment	Current Workpapers
11	Study of Controls — Sales and Cash Receipts	Current Workpapers
12	Tests of Controls and Substantive Tests of Transactions — Sales and Cash Receipts	Current Workpapers
13	Study of Controls — Acquisitions and Cash Disbursements	Current Workpapers
14	Tests of Controls and Substantive Tests of Transactions — Acquisitions and Cash Disbursements	Current Workpapers
	Tests of Balances	
20	Cash	Current Workpapers
21	Accounts and Notes Receivable	Current Workpapers
22	Inventories	Current Workpapers
23	Prepaid Expenses	Not included
24	Long-term Investments	Not included
25	Property, Plant, and Equipment	Not included
30	Accounts Payable	Current Workpapers
31	Accrued Liabilities	Not included
32	Notes and Loans Payable	Not included
33	Taxes Payable	Not included
34	Long-term Debt	Not included
35	Other Liabilities	Not included
40	Common Stock	Not included
41	Additional Paid-in Capital and Retained Earnings	Not included
	Completing the Audit	
90	Summary of Uncorrected Misstatements	Current Workpapers
91	Subsequent Events	Current Workpapers
92	Representation Letter	Current Workpapers
93	Management Letter	Current Workpapers

Section Number	Description	Location in this practice case
101	Client background information	Permanent file*
102	Chart of accounts	Permanent file
103	Client acceptance form	Permanent file
104	Organization chart	Permanent file
105	Appointment of auditor letter	Permanent file
106	Audit takeover letter and reply	Permanent file
107	Shareholder resolutions	Permanent file

The permanent file is located at the end of this booklet.

Each account balance on the financial statements is supported by workpapers organized into sections, beginning with section 20 (cash). Within each section, workpapers are arranged from general to specific. Each section begins with a leadsheet, which summarizes the balance(s) and adjustment(s) for that account(s). Each leadsheet is indexed as the first workpaper in each section (e.g., "20-1" for the cash leadsheet) and the pages following are sequenced in order: 20-2, 20-3, and so on.

Behind each leadsheet is the audit program. The audit program lists the procedures that are to be performed by the auditor and ends with a conclusion as to whether the account balance is fairly presented. Following the audit program are the workpapers that document the tests performed by the auditor.

Occasionally, an additional workpaper or workpapers must be inserted after indexing of a section is complete. Lilts Berger & Associates adds a lowercase letter to such workpapers, as follows: 20-1-a and 20-1-b. In the unlikely event that another workpaper needed to be inserted between workpaper 20-1-a and workpaper 20-1-b, it would be indexed as 20-1-a-i.

In the permanent file, workpapers are indexed as 101-1, 101-2, 102-1, 102-2, and so on.

Cross-referencing

Cross-referencing is used to indicate when one workpaper has information relevant for another workpaper. For example, the *cash in bank* balance on the cash leadsheet should be cross-referenced to the *adjusted balance per books* on the bank reconciliation. Some firms place the cross-reference on the right for a cross-reference *to* another workpaper and on the left to indicate a cross-reference *from* another workpaper. The location of the cross-reference is less important than making sure that each workpaper references the other workpaper.

Electronic workpapers in the Integrated Audit Practice Case

Most CPA firms use computers extensively in the audit process. Most firms perform "paperless audits" in which workpapers are created, completed, reviewed, and stored electronically.

In this practice case, paper copies of all workpapers needed to complete the case manually are provided in the *Workpaper* materials. However, use of a computer to complete the practice case provides efficiency advantages over completing the case manually.

Accordingly, many (but not all) of the workpapers are available in Microsoft Excel and Microsoft Word. See the E-materials at www.armonddaltonresources.com for steps to register on the Armond Dalton Resources website and download the project files. Microsoft Excel is used extensively by CPA firms in the audit process to create workpapers, financial statements, working trial balances, and to perform analytical procedures such as ratio and trend analysis.

Before beginning your work on the practice case, check with your instructor to determine which of the following three options you should use when completing the audit workpapers:

1. Complete all workpapers manually, ignoring the downloadable Excel and Word files.

2. Use a computer to complete the available electronic workpapers, print out copies of the workpapers as you complete them, and then submit the printouts to your instructor for grading.

3. Use a computer to complete the electronic workpapers, save the files with the completed workpapers, and submit the files to your instructor, along with the remaining workpapers completed manually to your instructor for grading. All electronic files can be submitted to your instructor online at www.armonddaltonresources.com (consult your instructor).

If you will be using option 1, you can ignore the rest of this section.

If you use options 2 or 3, you will need access to a computer, a printer, and Microsoft Excel and Word. In addition, you need a basic understanding of how to use Microsoft Excel and Microsoft Word.

> **NOTE:** To prevent accidental modifications of the Excel files, many of the cells have been "locked" and "protected." If you need to change any of these cells, you must first unprotect them by clicking REVIEW, UNPROTECT, SHEET.

Acknowledgments

We express our appreciation to CGA-Canada for permission to adapt materials from the CGA *Public Practice Manual* and the CGA *Practice Set 3*. This practice case has benefited significantly from the input of CGA-Canada.

There are several individuals who played key roles in designing, testing, and finalizing these materials. We are grateful for their contributions and efforts.

Carol Borsum, CPA. Carol is a CPA who spent eight years working on the audit staff of a large CPA firm. She spent hundreds of hours doing the entire case, making recommendations for revisions, and making certain that the materials and related workpapers are relevant and realistic.

Mark Beasley, Ph.D., CPA. Mark is a professor at North Carolina State University. He spent five years as a practicing auditor before becoming an Ernst & Young AICPA fellow and an AICPA technical staff manager for the Auditing Standards Board. His extensive and valuable comments have made a significant contribution to this practice case.

D. Dewey Ward, Ph.D. Our friend and colleague has used these materials in auditing courses many times and has provided significant guidance and suggestions for their improvement.

Steve Glover, Ph.D., CPA. Steve is a professor at Brigham Young University and has provided useful comments to help improve the case.

Ambrose Jones III, Ph.D., CPA. Ambrose is a professor at The University of North Carolina – Greensboro and has used the case several times and has provided several suggestions for the current and recent editions.

Nancy Schneider, MPA, CPA, CMA. Nancy, a professor at Lynchburg College, has used the case since its first edition. We appreciate the time she has taken to send us her comments and suggestions for improving the case.

Roberta Barra, Ph.D., CPA. Roberta is a professor at the University of Hawaii at Hilo and has provided helpful suggestions that have improved the case.

Regina Rexrode. Regina has provided invaluable assistance in formatting the materials. Her dedication, competence, perseverance, and cheerful attitude are greatly appreciated.

Patricia Naretta. Our publications would not be possible without Patti's careful and consistent copy editing and proofreading. Her hard work and professionalism contributed greatly to this case.

DSK
RJE
AAA

Assignments

Assignment 1: Review client background information

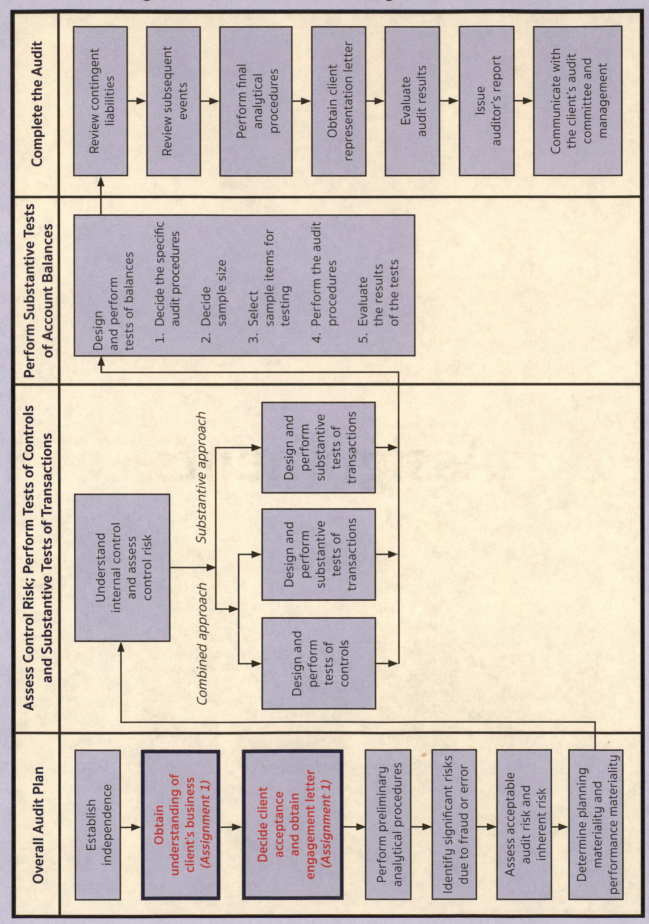

Complete the Audit
- Review contingent liabilities
- Review subsequent events
- Perform final analytical procedures
- Obtain client representation letter
- Evaluate audit results
- Issue auditor's report
- Communicate with the client's audit committee and management

Perform Substantive Tests of Account Balances

Design and perform tests of balances
1. Decide the specific audit procedures
2. Decide sample size
3. Select sample items for testing
4. Perform the audit procedures
5. Evaluate the results of the tests

Assess Control Risk; Perform Tests of Controls and Substantive Tests of Transactions

Understand internal control and assess control risk

Substantive approach

Combined approach

- Design and perform substantive tests of transactions
- Design and perform substantive tests of transactions
- Design and perform tests of controls

Overall Audit Plan
- Establish independence
- Obtain understanding of client's business *(Assignment 1)*
- Decide client acceptance and obtain engagement letter *(Assignment 1)*
- Perform preliminary analytical procedures
- Identify significant risks due to fraud or error
- Assess acceptable audit risk and inherent risk
- Determine planning materiality and performance materiality

ASSIGNMENT 1: Review client background information

Overview

In this assignment, you will:

- ⚓ review the client's background information and audit history.
- ⚓ review the CLIENT ACCEPTANCE FORM supporting the partners' decision to accept the engagement.
- ⚓ review the ENGAGEMENT LETTER.

Auditing concepts

Client acceptance

Before accepting a company as a new audit client, a CPA firm must establish whether it is independent and has the staff and expertise necessary to perform the audit. Before beginning the audit, the auditors must understand the company's business, industry, ownership, and management. If another public accounting firm previously audited the company, the successor auditor is required to communicate with the predecessor auditor. The purpose of this communication is for the predecessor auditor to have the opportunity to inform the successor auditor of any disagreements with the company over accounting issues, audit procedures, fees, or management's integrity. The successor CPA firm may also wish to contact the prospective client's banker and attorney to evaluate the company's acceptability. By performing all of these procedures, a CPA firm can reduce the risk of being associated with a client that the firm's partners would prefer not to serve. Unacceptable clients might include those with whom the risk of litigation is high, collection problems may arise, or client personnel are uncooperative.

Engagement letter

An engagement letter is the written agreement between a CPA firm and its client for the performance of an audit or related services. AICPA auditing standards (AU-C 210) indicate that the engagement letter includes the following information:

- *The objective and scope of the audit.* This normally includes the names and dates of the financial statements to be audited.
- *The responsibilities of the auditor.*
  - A statement informing the client that the audit will be performed in accordance with generally accepted auditing standards (or other auditing standards where applicable).
  - An audit is designed to provide reasonable assurance that the financial statements are free of material misstatement, whether due to fraud or error. The audit procedures performed depend on the auditor's judgment.
  - Due to the inherent limitation of an audit and the inherent limitation of internal control, an unavoidable risk exists that some material misstatements may not be detected.

- The auditor considers internal control in making risk assessments and designing audit procedures, but not for the purposes of expressing an opinion on the effectiveness of the entity's internal control.

- *Responsibilities of management.*
  - Management is responsible for the fair presentation of the financial statements in accordance with generally accepted accounting principles or other applicable accounting framework.
  - Management is responsible for the design, implementation, and maintenance of internal control relevant to preparation of the financial statements.
  - Management will provide access to information and written confirmation of the representations made during the audit.

- *Reporting.* Reference to the expected form and content of the audit report.

In addition, the engagement letter may also include:

- the fee arrangement, including method of billing and payment terms.
- description of additional services to be provided by the CPA firm, such as tax or management advisory services.
- further description of any assistance to be provided by the client during the engagement.

After reviewing the engagement letter, the client's officer or a member of the board of directors signs the letter and returns it to the CPA firm. The signed engagement letter represents the client's agreement with the terms of the engagement. The CPA firm retains the letter in its workpaper files or in a separate file. In this practice case, it is included in the current workpapers (see workpapers 4-1 through 4-3).

Requirements

a. If you have not already done so, read the guidelines for completing this practice case on pages 2 through 8 in the INTRODUCTION section of this booklet. Be sure to follow the *Guidelines for preparing audit documentation* on pages 2 and 3 in the *Introduction* section when completing each assignment.

Read the *Permanent file* included in the back of this booklet to become familiar with Oceanview Marine Company's background, operations, and audit history. Pay particular attention to factors that are most likely to affect a CPA firm's decision whether to accept Oceanview Marine Company as a client.

A critical part of client acceptance is establishing that the audit firm is independent from the audit client. Assume that Lilts Berger & Associates made the appropriate inquiries to establish that the firm is independent. This is documented in the CLIENT ACCEPTANCE FORM, question 24 (see workpaper 103-6 in the *Permanent File*).

Scan the unaudited financial statements for Oceanview Marine Company (workpapers 1-1 through 1-5), paying attention to any factors that might affect a CPA firm's decision whether to accept Oceanview Marine Company as a client.

b. Review the ENGAGEMENT LETTER for Oceanview Marine Company (workpapers 4-1 through 4-3).

The letter is missing two important sentences. Make any additions and changes that you believe are appropriate directly on the engagement letter (workpapers 4-1 through 4-3).

When finished, write your initials and date below CW's (Charles Ward, the audit engagement partner) initials on the top-right corner of each page of the engagement letter. Assume you are completing this procedure on 2/19/2019.

ELECTRONIC WORKPAPER OPTION: In this assignment, you can complete workpapers 4-1 through 4-3 in Microsoft Word. **These workpapers are included in the file named "Assign 1 Engagement Letter.docx."** If you use the electronic version of any of these workpapers, you may disregard the copy included in the *Current Workpapers*.

Completing the assignment

After you have completed this assignment, group the following items together in the order listed and submit them to your instructor for grading, either in person or online at armonddaltonresources.com (consult your instructor):

- Cover page with your printed name, your signature, and the assignment number.
- Engagement letter (workpapers 4-1 through 4-3).
- Answers to discussion questions 1 through 4 (see next two pages), if required by your instructor.

Discussion questions

1. Charles Ward, the engagement partner, has already completed the CLIENT ACCEPTANCE FORM in the permanent file. Based on the information you studied in the *Permanent File* and the unaudited financial statements included in the current workpapers (workpapers 1-1 through 1-5), evaluate the client acceptance decision. Organize your answer using the two-column format shown below.

   a. Indicate two favorable factors most important to the client acceptance decision (one factor has been provided as an example).
   b. Indicate three concerns you have about accepting Oceanview as a client.

Factors Favoring Acceptance	Concerns about Acceptance
1. Responses to inquiries of predecessor auditor were complimentary about Oceanview. Predecessor auditor spoke highly of Oceanview's employees' integrity, competence, and dedication to running a successful business.	1.
2.	2.
3.	3.

2. Indicate whether you agree with the decision to accept the client. Justify your decision, indicating the one or two factors from your response to the first question that had the greatest influence on your decision.

_____

_____

_____

_____

_____

_____

3. The client and our firm have agreed on an initial estimated audit fee of $32,000 (see the engagement letter). However, the estimated total cost of performing this year's audit is $37,590 (see the fee budget on workpaper 6-5). Discuss possible reasons why a CPA firm might charge a new client an audit fee that is *lower* than the estimated first-year costs of performing the audit.

_____

_____

_____

_____

_____

_____

_____

4. Auditing standards require auditors who are considering accepting an audit engagement to communicate with the previous auditors.

   a. What is the primary purpose of this communication between the new (successor) and old (predecessor) auditors?

   _____

   _____

   _____

   _____

   b. Why is the client's permission required before this communication can take place?

   _____

   _____

   _____

   _____

   c. The successor auditor also often reviews the predecessor auditor's workpapers. What is the primary purpose of reviewing these workpapers?

   _____

   _____

   _____

   _____

Assignment 2: Preliminary anaytical procedures and risk assessment discussion

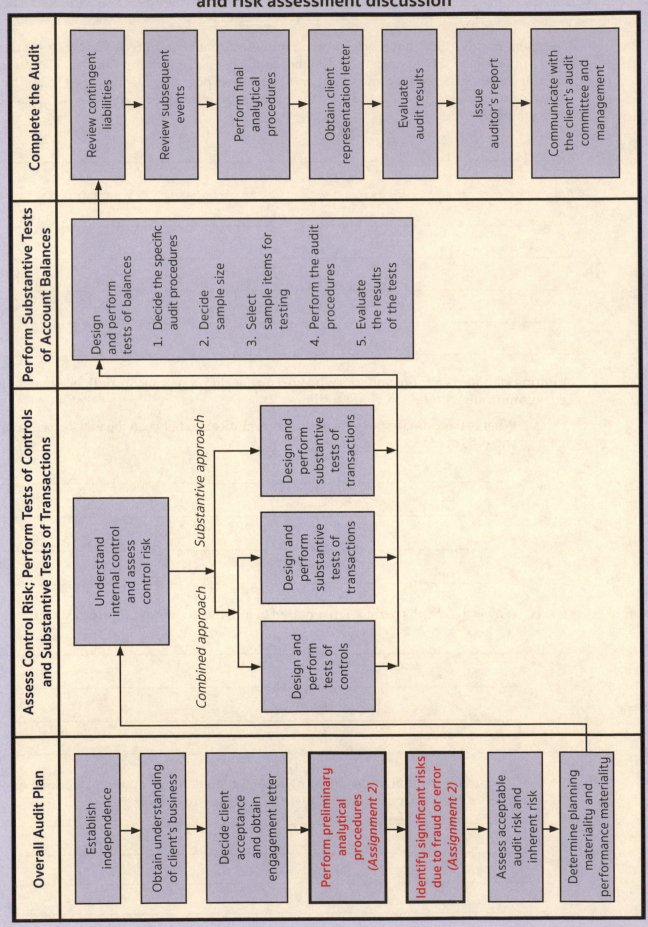

Complete the Audit
- Review contingent liabilities
- Review subsequent events
- Perform final analytical procedures
- Obtain client representation letter
- Evaluate audit results
- Issue auditor's report
- Communicate with the client's audit committee and management

Perform Substantive Tests of Account Balances

Design and perform tests of balances
1. Decide the specific audit procedures
2. Decide sample size
3. Select sample items for testing
4. Perform the audit procedures
5. Evaluate the results of the tests

Assess Control Risk; Perform Tests of Controls and Substantive Tests of Transactions

Understand internal control and assess control risk

Substantive approach

Combined approach

- Design and perform substantive tests of transactions
- Design and perform substantive tests of transactions
- Design and perform tests of controls

Overall Audit Plan
- Establish independence
- Obtain understanding of client's business
- Decide client acceptance and obtain engagement letter
- Perform preliminary analytical procedures (Assignment 2)
- Identify significant risks due to fraud or error (Assignment 2)
- Assess acceptable audit risk and inherent risk
- Determine planning materiality and performance materiality

ASSIGNMENT 2: Preliminary analytical procedures and risk assessment discussion

Overview

In this assignment you will:

⚓ perform an initial evaluation of Oceanview's financial condition.

⚓ perform preliminary analytical procedures to identify which account balances have increased risk of misstatement.

⚓ identify significant risks of material misstatement due to fraud or error as part of the risk assessment planning discussion.

Auditing concepts

Nature and use of analytical procedures

Auditing standards provide the following definition of analytical procedures:

> **Analytical procedures** are evaluations of financial information through analysis of plausible relationships among both financial and nonfinancial data. Analytical procedures also encompass such investigation, as is necessary, of identified fluctuations or relationships that are inconsistent with other relevant information or that differ from expected values by a significant amount.

Analytical procedures are used during various phases of an audit:

- planning phase
- substantive testing phase
- completion phase

Auditors are required to use analytical procedures during the planning phase of the audit as part of risk assessment procedures. Analytical procedures performed during the planning phase are often called **preliminary analytical procedures.**

Preliminary analytical procedures are used to identify accounts that may present a relatively high risk of misstatement. For example, comparisons of the current year's ending account balances with those of last year may reveal unexpected fluctuations. If the fluctuations are relatively large, the auditor investigates whether they are caused by misstatements or by valid business events.

Preliminary analytical procedures are also used to evaluate the client's financial condition. The client's financial condition affects audit risk and the amount of audit evidence required. In addition, the auditor must assess whether the company is likely to continue as a going concern for one year from the date of the financial statements. The evaluation of going concern is done near the end of the engagement. If the auditor has substantial doubt about the client's ability to continue, the auditor will modify the audit report.

The preliminary evaluation of the client's financial condition generally focuses on key financial ratios and trends in net income. For example, a lower than normal current ratio combined with a higher than normal debt-to-equity ratio and a declining trend in net income may suggest a relatively high risk of future financial difficulty. Ratio analyses are commonly performed to assess a company's liquidity, profitability, and solvency. **Liquidity** represents the company's ability to convert its assets to cash, which is needed to make day-to-day payments of bills and other debts. **Profitability** represents the company's ability to earn a profit (i.e., earnings), and profitability ratios measure how much the company is earning in relation to its assets, sales, or owners' equity. **Solvency** represents the company's ability to meet its debt obligations regardless of cash flow, and solvency ratios measure how much debt the company has in relation to its assets or owners' equity.

The auditor may obtain substantive evidence for relevant assertions from tests of details, substantive analytical procedures, or a combination of both. Substantive analytical procedures may be more efficient and effective than detailed substantive tests, depending on (a) the nature of the assertion, (b) the plausibility and predictability of the relationship, (c) the availability and reliability of the data used to develop the expectation, and (d) the precision of the expectation. For example, an auditor might compare the current year's ending balance in the "prepaid expenses" account with the prior year's audited ending balance. If the two amounts are roughly the same, the auditor may conclude that no additional audit work is necessary for that account, depending on its relative significance. The auditor should be alert, however, to any changes that may have occurred during the year in the client's policies regarding prepayments. Certain changes would lead the auditor to expect that the value of the current year's balance will be different than the previous year's balance.

In the completion phase of the audit, analytical procedures provide an overall review of the financial statements and assist the auditor in evaluating the appropriateness of the audit conclusions reached.

One of the most important aspects of analytical procedures is to investigate the cause of significant unexpected fluctuations in account balances or ratios. In addition, if certain fluctuations are expected but are not found, then the reason for the lack of fluctuations should be investigated. The logical starting point is to obtain and document an explanation from management. The auditor must then go beyond management's explanation and investigate whether or not the explanation is supported by audit evidence.

Risk assessment planning discussion

As part of risk assessment procedures performed during audit planning, the engagement team should engage in a discussion of where the financial statements may be susceptible to material misstatement, whether due to fraud or error. In addition, key engagement team members must participate in a brainstorming discussion of where the entity's financial statements might be susceptible to fraud. These two discussions are generally held concurrently.

Among other factors, the fraud risk discussion should address:

- known external and internal factors affecting the entity that may create an incentive or opportunity for management or others to commit fraud, provide the opportunity for fraud to be perpetrated, and indicate a culture or environment that enables management or others to rationalize committing fraud.

- the risk of management override of controls.
- the importance of maintaining professional skepticism throughout the audit.
- how the auditor might respond to the susceptibility of the entity's financial statements to material misstatement due to fraud.

Two types of fraud are *misappropriation of assets*, often called defalcation or employee fraud, and *fraudulent financial reporting*.

Auditors use the following framework, often referred to as the **"fraud triangle,"** to assess whether three conditions exist that increase the likelihood of fraud from fraudulent financial reporting and misappropriation of assets:

1. *Incentives/Pressures.* Management or other employees have incentives or pressures to commit fraud.
2. *Opportunities.* Circumstances provide opportunities for management or employees to commit fraud.
3. *Attitudes/Rationalization.* An attitude, character, or set of ethical values exist that allow management or employees to commit a dishonest act, or they are in an environment that imposes sufficient pressure that causes them to rationalize committing a dishonest act.

Requirements

a. In preparation for this assignment, obtain the following from the *Current Workpapers*:

- 2-1 through 2-5-b (*Current Workpapers—Audit Planning*)
- 93-1 and 93-2 (*Current Workpapers—Completing the Audit*)

These workpapers will be completed in this assignment and submitted to your instructor for grading. **Sign off** on each workpaper as you complete it, using 2/19/2019 as the completion date.

> **NOTE:** To sign off on a workpaper, write your initials and date in the top-right corner of the workpaper, below the index number. Your initials and date indicate: (1) that all the audit work related to that workpaper has been completed, (2) who completed the work, and (3) the date it was completed.

> **ELECTRONIC WORKPAPER OPTION:** In this assignment, you will complete and print workpaper 2-1 using Microsoft Excel. **This workpaper, along with workpapers 1-1 through 1-5 and 3-1 through 3-3 are included in the file named "Assign 2 and 10 Excel_7ed.xlsx."** You may disregard the copies of these workpapers in the Current Workpapers.
>
> To prevent accidental modifications of the Excel file, each sheet has been "protected." If you need to make changes to a sheet, you will need to first unprotect the sheet by clicking on Review, Unprotect Sheet.
>
> To switch between workpapers after you have opened the file in Excel, click on the sheet tabs on the bottom of the screen. If necessary, use the left and right arrows in the bottom-left corner of your screen to see all of the sheet tabs.

Assessment of client's financial condition

b. To assess the client's financial condition, Bill has calculated several liquidity, profitability/performance, and solvency ratios on workpaper 2-1. Complete the workpaper by calculating the remaining 2018 and 2017 values in each ratio category, including the change and percent change for each of the ratios. Round all ratios to two decimal places.

> **TIP:** To calculate the percent change from 2017 to 2018, divide column 3 (change) by column 2 (2017), not by column 1 (2018).

ELECTRONIC WORKPAPER OPTION: Complete and print workpaper 2-1 using Excel.

Use Excel to calculate the profitability ratios by dynamically "linking" the ratios in workpaper 2-1 to the related cells in the income statement and/or balance sheet (workpapers 1-1 and 1-2).

For instance, to determine the 2018 gross profit margin (rounded to two decimal places), you would input the following formula in cell B24 in Excel workpaper 2-1:

=round((‘income statement’!B10/’income statement’!B8),4)

Excel would then display 27.58%.

> **Note:** to round all subsequent ratios to two decimal places, use the round command as follows:

=round((*cell reference/cell reference*),2)

An important advantage of linking your ratios to the income statement and balance sheet is that the ratios are automatically updated if the income statement and/or balance sheet accounts are adjusted.

A second advantage is that you do not have to input the formulas for 2018 and 2017 separately; once you have entered the formulas for 2018, you can Copy and Paste the formulas to the 2017 column and Excel will adjust each formula and display the 2017 values for the ratios.

When calculating the Change and Percent Change, link columns D and E to columns B and C so the Change and Percent Change values will be updated if the income statement and/or balance sheet accounts are adjusted during the audit. For example, the Change and Percent Change for gross profit margin would be determined by inputting the following formulas in cells D24 and E24, respectively:

=B24-C24

=D24/C24

Before printing *Excel* sheets in this and all other assignments, you should disable the "print gridlines" option. Go to File, Print, click Page Setup, click the Sheet tab, and make sure the Gridlines box is not checked.

Print workpaper 2-1 when completed. You should **not** print the other workpapers in file **Assign 2 and 10 Excel 7ed.xlsx** at this time.

c. Study Oceanview Marine Company's current and prior years' financial ratios shown on workpaper 2-1. Also examine the industry data presented on workpaper 2-1.

On workpaper 2-2, add at least one more bullet commenting on the liquidity and solvency ratios. Complete the workpaper by writing a brief commentary on trends in the profitability ratios. Refer to reference materials as needed (textbooks, Internet sites on financial ratio analysis, etc.).

d. Based on your and Bill's analyses in step (c) above, and based on what you learned about the client in Assignment 1, complete the *Assessment of Financial Condition* workpaper (workpaper 2-3). Note that in assessing financial condition as part of performing preliminary analytical procedures, Lilts Berger & Associates assesses whether the client is likely to continue in business for the following two years.

Identification of accounts with unusual fluctuations

e. Review the common-size balance sheet and income statement (workpapers 2-6 and 2-7), noting accounts that may require follow-up with the client because of material unexpected fluctuations or lack of fluctuations where fluctuations were expected.

Use the top of workpaper 2-4-a to list two additional balance sheet accounts that you believe present the highest risks of misstatement requiring follow-up. Also state how each account balance differs from your expectations.

Use the bottom of workpaper 2-4-a to list three income statement accounts that you believe warrant follow-up due to unexpected fluctuations or lack of fluctuations where fluctuations were expected. Also state how each account balance differs from your expectations.

> **TIP:** Remember that you want to identify material unexpected fluctuations. For example, if an expense account increases from $100 in the prior year to $200 in the current year, the change is unexpected, but is likely not material. Similarly, an expense account may reflect a material increase in dollars compared to the prior year. However, if the expense is expected to vary with sales and the expense as a percentage of sales has remained fairly constant, the change is not unexpected.

f. Review each of the divisional income statements (workpapers 2-8 through 2-12), noting any significant fluctuations that should be investigated and discussed with the client.

Use workpaper 2-4-b to list the three divisional accounts that you believe are most likely to be misstated as indicated by unexpected fluctuations or lack of fluctuation where expected. Also state how each account balance differs from your expectations.

> **NOTE:** If possible, identify significant divisional fluctuations for the **same** accounts you identified in step e, and identify, in column one of workpaper 2-4-b, **which division** is most responsible for the income statement fluctuation you identified in step e.

> **NOTE:** As you analyze the divisional common-size income statements as well as the combined common-size income statement, you may find that the divisional statements reveal underlying trends and fluctuations not apparent in the combined income statement.

g. You have been invited to attend the risk assessment planning discussion. Bill has identified on workpaper 2-5-a a significant risk of material misstatement for revenue. Based on your knowledge of the client gained in Assignment 1 and your preliminary analytical procedures, identify at least two additional accounts where you believe there is a significant risk of material misstatement.

For each account (except Sales), complete the section labeled "Nature of potential material misstatement." To do this, you should consider possible significant misstatements given the nature of the client's business and the results of your preliminary analytical procedures. Indicate below the potential misstatement whether or not you believe it represents a significant fraud risk.

For each account (except Sales), complete the section labeled "Effect on audit procedures." To do this, you should suggest audit tests that could be used later in the audit to determine whether the year-end balance in the account is misstated. Bill has already completed this section for Sales.

h.   Because this is a first-year audit, your firm is anxious to impress the client by sending a management letter with suggestions that will improve Oceanview's operations by increasing operational efficiency, improving financial condition, or reducing taxes.

On workpapers 93-1 and 93-2, provide at least two such suggestions for Oceanview's management. Your recommendations should be drafted in this format: (i) problem or area for improvement, (ii) why adopting a change is important, (iii) your suggestion and plan of implementation.

> **TIP:** You should base your management letter recommendations primarily on the analytical procedures you performed in this assignment and on your understanding of the client gained in Assignment 1. In addition, recommendations can be based on concepts learned in other accounting and business courses such as finance, management, and marketing. For example, you may have a recommendation concerning the client's financing based on concepts learned in your finance course(s).
>
> See Bill's comment #1 on workpaper 93-1 for an example. (Bill's comments #1 through #4 are based on work he performed prior to his re-assignment.)

Completing the assignment

Make sure you **signed off** on each workpaper that you completed in this assignment (2-1 through 2-5-b, and 93-1), using 2/19/2019 as the completion date. Do not sign off on workpaper 93-2 yet, since it has not been completed; i.e., you will be adding additional items to that workpaper in subsequent assignments.

Group the following items together in the order listed and submit them to your instructor for grading, either in person or online at armonddaltonresources.com (consult your instructor):

- Cover page with your printed name, your signature, and the assignment number.
- Workpapers 2-1 through 2-3, 2-4-a, 2-4-b, 2-5-a, and 2-5-b.
- Workpapers 93-1 and 93-2.
- Answers to discussion questions 1 through 5 (see next two pages) if required by your instructor.

Discussion questions

1. AICPA auditing standards require a discussion among the engagement team about the susceptibility of the financial statements to material misstatement. What are some of the purposes of this discussion?

_____

_____

_____

_____

_____

_____

2. The auditor reviews important financial statement numbers and ratios at both the beginning and the completion of the audit. Compare and contrast the purposes of (1) preliminary analytical procedures and (2) analytical procedures performed near the completion of the audit.

_____

_____

_____

_____

_____

_____

3. When you identified income statement fluctuations in steps (e) and (f) of this assignment, which information did you find most helpful — comparisons of the current year's and prior year's balances, or comparisons of the current year's and prior year's balances as a percentage of sales? Explain.

_____

_____

_____

_____

_____

_____

4. The auditor should consider the results of analytical procedures performed in planning the audit that indicate possible implausible or unexpected relationships in assessing the risk of fraud. For example, if the auditor compares revenue reported by product line each month (i.e., monthly sales volume) with sales (or production) capacity, and determines that the number of items reported as sold exceeds capacity, then the auditor should be concerned that revenue may be materially overstated due to fraudulent revenue transactions. What other types of unexpected relationships, ratios, or trends might suggest an increased risk of fraud? Discuss any relationships, ratios, or trends you identified in this assignment that might represent an increased fraud risk.

_____

_____

_____

_____

_____

_____

5. The client's "going concern" status is an audit reporting issue that is addressed at the conclusion of the audit. Auditing standards require the auditor to assess whether the client is likely to continue in existence for a reasonable period of time after the date of the financial statements. Indicate reasons why the auditor should also address the company's going concern status in the *planning* stage of the audit.

_____

_____

_____

_____

_____

_____

Assignment 3: Determine materiality and assess risks

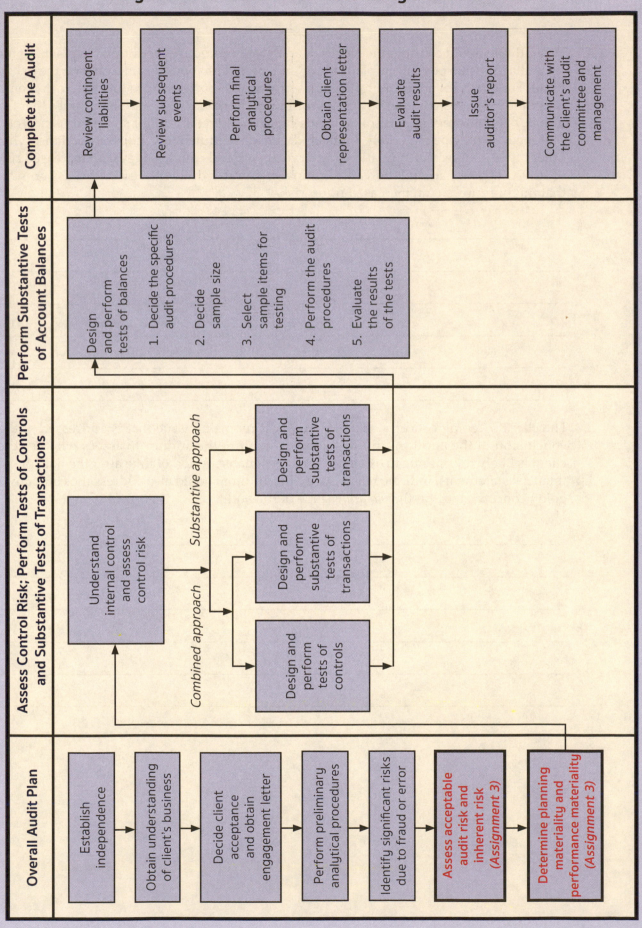

Complete the Audit
- Review contingent liabilities
- Review subsequent events
- Perform final analytical procedures
- Obtain client representation letter
- Evaluate audit results
- Issue auditor's report
- Communicate with the client's audit committee and management

Perform Substantive Tests of Account Balances

Design and perform tests of balances
1. Decide the specific audit procedures
2. Decide sample size
3. Select sample items for testing
4. Perform the audit procedures
5. Evaluate the results of the tests

Assess Control Risk; Perform Tests of Controls and Substantive Tests of Transactions

Understand internal control and assess control risk

Substantive approach
- Design and perform substantive tests of transactions

Combined approach
- Design and perform substantive tests of transactions
- Design and perform tests of controls

Overall Audit Plan
- Establish independence
- Obtain understanding of client's business
- Decide client acceptance and obtain engagement letter
- Perform preliminary analytical procedures
- Identify significant risks due to fraud or error
- Assess acceptable audit risk and inherent risk *(Assignment 3)*
- Determine planning materiality and performance materiality *(Assignment 3)*

ASSIGNMENT 3: Determine materiality and assess acceptable audit risk and inherent risk

Overview

In this assignment you will:

- ⚓ study Oceanview Marine Company's business.
- ⚓ decide an acceptable level of audit risk for the audit of Oceanview.
- ⚓ determine an appropriate materiality level for the audit.
- ⚓ assess the level of inherent risk associated with specific balance sheet accounts.
- ⚓ determine performance materiality for specific balance sheet accounts.

The assessment of acceptable audit risk, the preliminary judgment about materiality, the determination of performance materiality, and assessments of inherent risk are decisions the auditor makes when planning the audit.

Auditing concepts

Acceptable level of audit risk

Audit risk is the risk that the auditor will issue an unmodified audit opinion on financial statements that are materially misstated. As shown in the equation below, audit risk is a combination of (1) the risk that a material misstatement will occur in an account (inherent risk), (2) the risk that the client's internal controls will not prevent or detect the misstatement (control risk), and (3) the risk that the auditor will not detect the misstatement (detection risk). The auditor reduces audit risk to an acceptable level by performing substantive tests, which reduce detection risk.

Audit risk = Inherent risk x Control risk x Detection risk

Auditors use the audit risk model to help plan how much evidence to gather during the audit. The auditor normally begins by determining an "acceptable" ("allowable" or "target") level of audit risk. Acceptable audit risk is typically assessed as high, moderate, or low. Generally speaking, when acceptable audit risk is low, more substantive testing will need to be done during the audit than when acceptable audit risk is moderate or high. Acceptable audit risk is the inverse of audit assurance. A low acceptable audit risk requires a high level of audit assurance.

The primary factor the auditor considers when determining an acceptable level of audit risk is the likelihood that, sometime in the future, the auditor may be required to defend the quality of the audit (i.e., the likelihood of being sued). This likelihood, in turn, is influenced by three factors:

1. The extent to which users of the financial statements will rely on those statements.
2. The likelihood that the client may experience financial trouble in the near future.
3. Management's integrity.

The extent of users' reliance on financial statements is influenced by several conditions, including:

- *Future public offering, merger, or sale of the company.* The financial statements of a company that is about to go public, merge, or be sold will be relied on heavily by potential buyers/investors. This reduces the amount of audit risk the auditor is willing to accept; i.e., acceptable audit risk.
- *Ownership of the client.* Generally, more people will rely on the financial statements of widely held public companies than those of closely-held or private companies. The larger the ownership, the lower the auditor's acceptable level of audit risk.
- *Extent of debt.* Creditors rely on financial statements to decide whether to grant credit or expand loans. The more the company is leveraged, the lower the auditor's acceptable level of audit risk.
- *Size of the client.* The financial statements of larger companies will generally be relied on by more people than statements of smaller companies. Thus, when auditing larger companies, the auditor generally seeks to achieve relatively low levels of audit risk.

In assessing the likelihood that a company will experience financial difficulty or failure, the auditor should consider:

- profitability and solvency
- competence of management
- industry in which the company operates
- capital structure

The following chart illustrates the risk factors and their effects on acceptable audit risk:

Risk factors: (one or more may be relevant)	Acceptable audit risk will be relatively high	Acceptable audit risk will be moderate/normal	Acceptable audit risk will be relatively low
1. Extent of reliance on financial statements	Financial statements are used primarily ✓ internally by management. Client is probably privately owned (low reliance).	Financial statements are used primarily by management for normal business loans. Client could be either privately or publicly owned (moderate reliance).	Client is a widely held public company or is about to go public or be sold (financial statements will be relied on heavily by external users).
2. Likelihood of financial difficulty	Low likelihood of financial difficulty.	Low to moderate ✓ likelihood of financial difficulty.	Moderate to high likelihood of financial failure in near future.
3. Management integrity	Management has ✓ high integrity.	Management has reasonably high integrity.	Management's integrity is low.

Preliminary judgment about materiality

An auditor's preliminary judgment about materiality (also called planning materiality) reflects the largest amount by which the financial statements could be misstated without affecting the decisions of a person relying on the financial statements. For example, the auditor might conclude for a given audit that net income before taxes could be misstated by as much as ±3 to 10% without materially affecting the fair presentation of the financial statements.

Determining preliminary materiality involves professional judgment, and usually involves applying an appropriate percentage to an appropriate base. In normal circumstances, net income before taxes is generally the appropriate base for for-profit entities, although other bases may be used depending on the nature of the client. See Lilts Berger & Associates' POLICY STATEMENT included in this assignment for a description of the firm's policies regarding the preliminary judgment about materiality.

Performance materiality

The preliminary judgment about materiality applies to the financial statements as a whole. Performance materiality is the amount or amounts set by the auditor at an amount less than materiality for the financial statements as a whole for particular classes of transactions, account balances, or disclosures. The auditor assesses performance materiality to determine the nature, timing, and extent of further audit procedures.

Performance materiality should be assessed to reduce, to an appropriately low level, the probability that the aggregate of uncorrected and undetected misstatements exceeds materiality for the financial statements as a whole. Some firms assess performance materiality for each account as a fixed percentage, such as 50% or 75% of the preliminary judgment about materiality. Other firms specify an amount of performance materiality for each account.

Several factors affect the size of the auditor's performance materiality for individual accounts. Performance materiality is usually set lower for account balances that have no expected misstatements and can be audited at minimal cost, such as cash or notes payable. Performance materiality is usually set higher for account balances that have a high number about expected misstatements or are difficult to audit, such as inventory or accounts receivable.

The combined performance materiality for all accounts will normally exceed the preliminary judgment about materiality because (1) it is highly unlikely that each account will be misstated by the full amount of its performance materiality, and (2) there may be offsetting misstatements as some accounts are overstated while others are understated. As a result, however, it is possible that when the audit is completed, the combined estimated misstatement for all accounts might exceed the preliminary judgment about materiality, even though no account is misstated by more than its performance materiality. If that occurs, the auditor must accumulate additional evidence in certain accounts or request that the client adjust the financial statements.

Inherent risk

Inherent risk is the risk of a material misstatement in an account before considering the effectiveness of internal control. Inherent risk is assessed for each relevant assertion. The combined assessment of inherent risk and control risk is the **risk of material misstatement** in the financial statements and consists of:

- risk related to the nature of the account or transaction (inherent risk)
- risk related to the client's internal control (control risk)

Early in the audit, the auditor assesses inherent risk and control risk. The purpose of assessing risk early is to help the auditor plan the audit by deciding which parts of the audit to emphasize and deciding the extent of testing. In developing these assessments of risk, the auditor considers the nature of the client's business and industry and whether client business risk is associated with increased likelihood of material misstatements in the financial statements. The auditor should examine more extensively those accounts that are most likely to contain material misstatements and examine less extensively those accounts that are least likely to be materially misstated. For example, inventory usually is associated with high inherent risk because it is susceptible to theft, numerous transactions affect inventory in each period, numerous calculations are needed to determine the inventory's year-end valuation, and the dollar amount of the account is usually large. In contrast, prepaid insurance usually has less inherent risk because it is less susceptible to theft, it involves relatively few transactions, calculations to determine prepaid insurance are relatively simple, and the dollar amount involved is relatively small. Even when material misstatements are unlikely, some substantive testing is usually necessary for material accounts; however, the extent of testing can be less than when material misstatements are likely.

The following factors are likely to cause an account's inherent risk to be high:

- The account balance is large.
- The account consists of a large number of transactions.
- The account comprises large individual transactions.
- The account comprises unusual or difficult transactions requiring professional judgment or technical expertise to record properly or is based on subjectively determined estimates.
- Several steps are involved from the initiation of a transaction to its posting in the general ledger.
- The assets are highly susceptible to theft.
- There is major motivation by management to "window dress" or misstate the financial statements.
- Management has low integrity.
- There are related-party transactions affecting the account.
- Material misstatements were discovered in the account during the previous year's audit.

A portion of this assignment focuses on identifying factors affecting inherent risk. The predecessor auditors of Oceanview Marine Company have indicated to your firm that last year's audit revealed no material misstatements in Oceanview's accounting records. Therefore, you will begin this assignment by assuming a relatively low risk of misstatements and proceed by identifying and documenting any high-risk factors you believe are present.

LILTS BERGER & ASSOCIATES, CPAs
Ocean City, Florida

POLICY STATEMENT

Title: Materiality Guidelines—Preliminary Judgment about Materiality and Performance Materiality

Preliminary Judgment about Materiality

Professional judgment is to be used at all times in setting and applying materiality guidelines. Materiality must be measured in relation to the appropriate base. As a general guideline, the following policies are to be applied:

1. For profit-oriented companies, the appropriate materiality base will be pre-tax income. The preliminary judgment about materiality should ordinarily be measured between 5 and 10% of net income before taxes for private companies. A combined total of misstatements or omissions in the financial statements exceeding 10% is normally considered material. A combined total of less than 5% is presumed to be immaterial in the absence of qualitative factors. Combined misstatements or omissions between 5 and 10% require the greatest amount of professional judgment to determine their materiality. Acceptable audit risk is a major consideration in the decision. When acceptable audit risk is low, the preliminary judgment about materiality would typically be 5 to 6% of pre-tax income. When acceptable audit risk is high, the preliminary judgment about materiality would be 9 to 10% of pre-tax income.

    [handwritten margin notes: <5% immaterial; >10% material; 5~10% judgment necessary]

    If net income before taxes in a given year is not considered representative (unusually high, low, or negative), it would be desirable to use a different base such as total assets (see 2 below).

2. Often there is more than one base to which misstatements could be compared. Normalized pre-tax income may not be an appropriate base for not-for-profit enterprises.

    Also, if a company operates in an industry where size is more relevant than operations or where net income before taxes is unusually low or high for the size of the company, the preliminary judgment about materiality should be measured using either balance sheet or income statement amounts as a base. Even if the preliminary judgment about materiality is based on pretax income, a balance sheet-based calculation is useful for evaluating the materiality of misclassifications between balance sheet accounts. For total assets, the guidelines should be between ½ and 1% of assets.

3. Qualitative factors should be carefully evaluated in the final evaluation of materiality on all audits. In many instances, they are more important than the guidelines applied to the income statement and balance sheet. The intended uses of the financial statements and the nature of the information in the statements, including footnotes, must be carefully evaluated.

Performance Materiality

Professional judgment is to be used in setting and applying performance materiality. As a general guideline, the following policies are to be applied:

1. Performance materiality will be established only for balance sheet accounts.
2. Performance materiality will be established for every balance sheet account except retained earnings.
3. The maximum performance materiality to be applied to any account is 75% of the preliminary judgment about materiality.
4. The combined performance materiality for all accounts shall not exceed three times the preliminary judgment about materiality.
5. The following are major factors affecting the setting of performance materiality for individual balance sheet accounts:
    - Performance materiality should be set higher for accounts with a high cost to audit (i.e., larger accounts, and accounts that are relatively difficult to audit).
    - Performance materiality, as a percent of the account balance, should be set higher for accounts with a higher expectation of misstatement.

Requirements

a. In preparation for this assignment, obtain the following from the *Current Workpapers*: 5-1a through 5-4.

These workpapers will be completed in this assignment and submitted to your instructor for grading. **Sign off** on each workpaper as you complete it, using 2/22/2019 as the completion date.

> **ELECTRONIC WORKPAPER OPTION:** In this assignment, you can complete and print workpapers 5-1-a/b and 5-2-a/b (**file names Wp 5-1a and b.docx and Wp 5-2a and b.docx**). You can complete and print workpapers 5-3 and 5-4 using Microsoft Excel (**file name Assign3 Excel_7ed.xlsx**). If you use the electronic version of any of these workpapers, you may disregard the copy included in the *Current Workpapers*.

Decision about the acceptable level of audit risk

b. Use workpapers 5-1-a and 5-1-b to decide and document the acceptable level of audit risk for the audit of Oceanview Marine Company.

> **TIP:** Your assessment of the Likelihood of Financial Difficulty on workpaper 5-1-a should be consistent with your assessment on workpaper 2-3. Cross reference workpaper 5-1-a to workpaper 2-3 by writing "2-3" next to "Source W/P reference" in section A on workpaper 5-1-a (see the discussion of cross referencing on page 6 in the INTRODUCTION section of this booklet).
>
> When completing sections B, C, and D on workpaper 5-1-a, you may want to review the CLIENT BACKGROUND INFORMATION AND CLIENT ACCEPTANCE FORM in the *Permanent file* (workpapers 101-1 to 101-3, and 103-1 to 103-8).

Preliminary judgment about materiality

c. Use workpaper 5-2-a to make a preliminary estimate of the materiality level for the Oceanview audit (round your materiality level to the next lowest $5,000).

> **TIP:** To complete section 2 of workpaper 5-2-a, use your CPA firm's POLICY STATEMENT included with this assignment to help you choose an appropriate base and percentage.

d. On workpaper 5-2-b, explain and support your choice of the base and percentage for determining materiality.

> **TIP:** When explaining your choice of percentage, link it to your earlier assessment of acceptable audit risk (i.e., state your acceptable level of audit risk and how it influenced your choice of the percentage).

Assessment of inherent risk

e. Use workpaper 5-3 to assess inherent risk for accounts receivable, allowance for doubtful accounts, inventory, prepaid expenses, property, plant and equipment, and accounts payable. Bill Cullen has completed the assessment of inherent risk for each of the other accounts on workpaper 5-3.

> **ELECTRONIC WORKPAPER OPTION:** Complete and print workpaper 5-3 using Excel.

Allocation of materiality—performance materiality

f. On workpaper 5-4, complete the Performance Materiality column to establish performance materiality for each balance sheet account. Bill has already established performance materiality for several of the accounts. Follow the guidelines provided in the bottom section of your firm's POLICY STATEMENT included with this assignment to establish performance materiality for each of the remaining accounts. In making your allocations, you should attempt to allocate the maximum total allowable allocation of three times your preliminary materiality level.

Complete the bottom portion of workpaper 5-4 and make sure that your total performance materiality does not exceed the maximum allowable allocation of three times your preliminary materiality level.

> **ELECTRONIC WORKPAPER OPTION:** Complete and print workpaper 5-4 using Excel.

Review of audit planning checklist and audit budgets

g. Bill Cullen completed the audit-planning checklist and prepared the time and fee budgets for the Oceanview Marine Company engagement (see workpapers 6-1 through 6-5).

Study these workpapers to familiarize yourself with the audit planning process and the issues addressed therein.

Completing the assignment

Make sure you **signed off** on all workpapers included in Section 5 of the *Current Workpapers*, using 2/22/2019 as the date.

Group the following items together in the order listed and submit them to your instructor for grading, either in person or online at armonddaltonresources.com (consult your instructor):

- Cover page with your printed name, your signature, and the assignment number.
- Workpapers 5-1 through 5-4.
- Answers to discussion questions 1 through 5 (see next two pages) if required by your instructor.

Discussion questions

1. Explain why decisions about acceptable audit risk, inherent risk, the preliminary judgment about materiality, and performance materiality should be made early in the audit during the planning phase.

_____

_____

_____

_____

_____

_____

2. Explain how the levels of acceptable audit risk and preliminary materiality you selected in this assignment might affect the remainder of the audit. Specifically, what effect would *lower* levels of acceptable audit risk and materiality have on audit testing compared to the levels you selected?

_____

_____

_____

_____

_____

_____

3. Why is net income before tax the most common base used to determine the preliminary judgment about materiality? In what circumstances might the auditor use a different base?

_____

_____

_____

_____

_____

_____

_____

4. In requirement (f) of this assignment, you established performance materiality for each of several balance sheet accounts. Explain/justify how you chose your performance materiality amounts for each of the following accounts: (a) accounts receivable, (b) allowance for bad debts, (c) accounts payable.

_____

_____

_____

_____

_____

_____

_____

5. Explain/justify why the sum of performance materiality is allowed to exceed the preliminary judgment about materiality.

_____

_____

_____

_____

_____

_____

_____

Assignment 4: Assess control risk and plan tests of controls and substantive tests of transactions

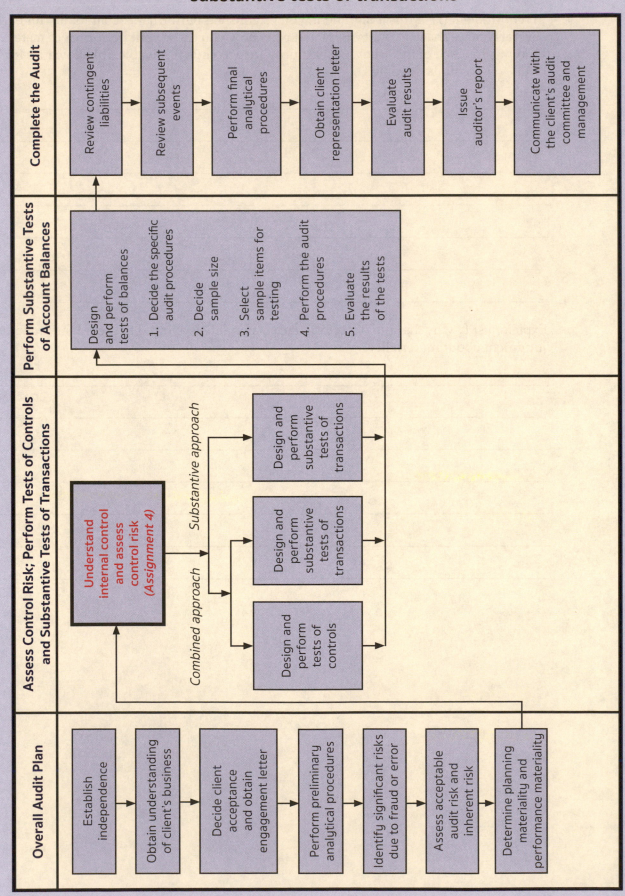

ASSIGNMENT 4: Assess control risk and plan tests of controls and substantive tests of transactions

Overview

In this assignment you will:

- ⚓ gain an understanding of Oceanview Marine Company's internal controls.
- ⚓ assess Oceanview Marine Company's control environment.
- ⚓ make a preliminary assessment of control risk for acquisitions.
- ⚓ plan tests of controls and substantive tests of transactions for acquisitions.

Auditing concepts

Internal Control

Internal Control—Integrated Framework published by the Committee of Sponsoring Organizations of the Treadway Commission (COSO) states that an organization's internal control provides reasonable assurance regarding achievement of objectives related to (1) financial reporting, (2) operations, and (3) compliance with rules and regulations.

Auditing standards describe the following five components of a company's internal control:

1. *The control environment*. The control environment is the foundation of the other components of internal control, and reflects management's attitude toward internal control. These factors include:

   - management's philosophy and operating style
   - organizational structure
   - assignment of authority and responsibility
   - management control methods
   - participation by the audit committee or those charged with governance
   - internal audit function
   - personnel policies and procedures, including commitment to competence.

2. *Risk assessment*. This is the client's identification, analysis, and management of risks relevant to the preparation of financial statements.

3. *Control activities*. These are the policies and procedures that help ensure that the company's objectives are achieved. Examples of specific control activities include:
   - adequate segregation of duties
   - proper authorization of transactions
   - adequate documents and records
   - physical controls over documents and assets
   - independent reviews and checks on performance

4. *Information and communication*. The client's information system, which includes the accounting system, consists of the methods and records established to record, process, summarize, and report transactions and to maintain accountability for the company's assets, liabilities, and equity.

5. *Monitoring*. Monitoring involves management's ongoing assessment of whether the system of internal control is operating effectively.

Understand the client's internal controls

Auditing standards indicate the auditor must obtain a sufficient understanding of the entity and its environment, including its internal control, to assess the risk of material misstatement of the financial statements whether due to fraud or error, and to design the nature, timing, and extent of further audit procedures. The auditor's study of the client's internal controls is accomplished primarily through inquiries of the client, observation of the client's activities, and inspection of the client's documents and electronic records.

As part of the study of the client's internal controls, the auditor documents his/her understanding of the process for initiating, authorizing, recording, processing, and recording transactions, including the design of relevant internal controls for each assertion in the audit workpapers. This documentation usually takes one or more of the following forms:

- flowcharts showing the flow of documents through the accounting system and the related control activities
- narrative (written) descriptions of the client's internal controls
- internal control questionnaires related to the internal controls

In addition to understanding the design of internal controls, the auditor should verify that the controls have been implemented. This is usually accomplished by a **walkthrough**, in which an auditor follows a single transaction from its initiation to its recording in the accounting records. In addition to examining the completed documents and records, the auditor makes inquiries of client personnel and observes the performance of client activities.

Assess control risk

Once the auditor has obtained and documented an understanding of the client's internal controls, he/she then makes an initial assessment of control risk. Control risk represents the likelihood that the internal controls will neither prevent material misstatements from occurring nor detect and correct misstatements if they do occur. Control risk is assessed for each relevant financial statement assertion, or alternatively, the related audit objectives. For example, an auditor may believe that controls relating to sales transactions are effective in preventing the recording of fictitious sales (*existence or occurrence* assertion) but are weak in preventing omissions in the recording of sales transactions (*completeness* assertion). Accordingly, the auditor would initially assess control risk for the *existence or occurrence* of sales as low and control risk for the *completeness* of sales as high.

Whenever the auditor's preliminary assessment of control risk is less than the maximum level (i.e., he/she believes the controls can be relied upon to some extent), the auditor must perform tests of the controls to support that initial assessment. Tests of controls are used to determine whether the controls operated effectively throughout the period under audit.

After the auditor has performed the tests of controls, he/she makes a final assessment of control risk. If the results of the tests of controls indicate that the controls operated effectively, final control risk can be assessed at some level less than 100%. However, if tests of controls reveal that the controls have not been operating satisfactorily, then control risk would be assessed at 100% (i.e., high) for the assertions and/or objectives associated with those controls.

After making the final assessment of control risk, the auditor uses that assessment, along with the audit risk model, to determine the appropriate extent of substantive testing for each balance sheet and income statement account affected.

Plan tests of controls

The design of the tests of controls depends on two things: the internal controls identified in the auditor's study of internal control and the preliminary assessment of control risk.

If the auditor has identified a control that he/she intends to rely on to reduce control risk, one or more tests of controls should be performed to determine if the control is functioning properly. Here is an example:

Control:	Test of Control:
Purchase orders are properly authorized.	Examine a sample of purchase orders for indication of proper authorization.

Plan substantive tests of transactions

The primary distinction between tests of controls and substantive tests of transactions is that tests of controls are used to gain assurance that internal controls are operating effectively, whereas substantive tests of transactions are used to gain assurance that the data produced by the accounting system are accurate. If control risk is assessed at less than 100%, substantive tests of transactions are often combined with tests of controls.

For most audits, the account balances related to the acquisition of goods and services and cash disbursements are:

- cash
- inventory
- prepaids and accruals
- property, plant, and equipment
- accounts payable
- most operating expenses

Substantive tests of balances for some or all of these accounts can be reduced if:

- the auditor concludes that controls are effective after performing tests of controls and/or
- the auditor concludes that transactions are correctly recorded after performing substantive tests of transactions.

It is best to design substantive tests of transactions on an objective-by-objective basis to be sure that sufficient, but not excessive, tests are performed for each audit objective. The planned tests of controls often affect the planned substantive tests of transactions because both are normally applied to the same sample of transactions. Here is the usual decision process:

1. Decide which controls will be tested.
2. Design the appropriate tests of controls for each control identified in step 1.
3. Associate controls to be tested and related tests of controls with financial statement assertions and related audit objectives. (Note that a control may satisfy more than one objective.)
4. Design substantive tests of transactions for each objective, depending on the amount of evidence you plan to obtain from these tests.

Background information

Bill Cullen met several times with Cynthia—Oceanview's controller—and other accounting personnel to obtain information about Oceanview's internal control, including the control environment, the accounting system (information and communication), and control activities. Bill has partially completed the assessment of the overall level of control in the control environment. He has completed the preliminary assessment of control risk for sales and has planned the tests of controls and substantive tests of transactions for sales.

Your assignment will be to (1) assess the overall level of control in the control environment, (2) complete the preliminary assessment of control risk for acquisitions, and (3) plan the tests of controls and substantive tests of transactions for acquisitions.

Requirements

a. In preparation for this assignment, obtain the following from the *Current Workpapers:* 10-8, 13-1, 13-3, 13-4, 14-1, and 14-2.

These workpapers will be completed in this assignment and turned in to your instructor for grading. Remember to sign off on each workpaper as you complete it. Use 2/23/2019 as the completion date for each workpaper you complete in this assignment.

> **ELECTRONIC WORKPAPER OPTION:** In this assignment, you can complete and print workpapers 10-8, 13-3, 13-4, 14-1, and 14-2 using Microsoft Word. **These workpapers are included in the file named "Assign 4 Word_7ed."** If you use the electronic version of any of these workpapers, you may disregard the copy included in the *Current Workpapers*.

b. On workpaper 10-8, complete number 1 to assess the level of control in Oceanview Marine Company's control environment. Include workpaper references in the "comments" column.

> **TIP:** Workpaper 10-8 summarizes the results of the control environment questionnaire (workpapers 10-1 through 10-7) to enable you to make an overall assessment of the control environment.
>
> To complete workpaper 10-8, you will need to study workpapers 10-1 through 10-7.
>
> Numbers 2 through 4 on workpaper 10-8 have been completed to provide you with examples of how to fill in number 1. For instance, the "comments" section of number 4 refers to workpaper 10-7 on the IT (Information Technology) department. The control level has been assessed as ineffective because, as indicated on workpaper 10-7, segregation of functions between the IT department and users is lacking.

c. Complete the "Conclusions" section of workpaper 10-8 by stating whether the control environment appears to be effective or ineffective. Your conclusion should be based on whether the majority of your assessments in the summary indicate that the controls exist. (Note that due to the relatively small size of Oceanview, the absence of an internal audit department or audit committee does not automatically mean that the control environment is ineffective.)

d. Bill Cullen has completed the preliminary assessment of control risk for sales (workpapers 11-1 through 11-4). Study those workpapers to familiarize yourself with the client's accounting system and internal controls over sales.

Bill has partially completed the audit program for the evaluation of internal control over acquisitions (workpaper 13-1). Complete step 5 on the audit program and, when completed, fill in the columns for your initials, date, and workpaper reference.

> **TIP:** Complete the internal control questionnaire on workpaper 13-3 using the flowchart on workpaper 13-2 as your source of information. In the "remarks" column on workpaper 13-3, indicate the name of the person, if applicable, who performs each internal control procedure.
>
> Use workpaper 11-3 as a guide, if necessary.

e. Complete step 6 on the audit program (workpaper 13-1). When completed, fill in the columns for your initials, date, and workpaper reference.

> **TIP:** The "Preliminary Assessment of Control Risk—Acquisitions" matrix referred to in step 6 is found on workpaper 13-4.
>
> Use workpaper 13-3 to identify the client's existing controls and deficiencies.
>
> Use workpapers 11-1 through 11-4 as a guide, if necessary.

f. Bill Cullen designed the tests of controls for sales and the substantive tests of sales transactions (workpapers 12-1 and 12-2). Study these workpapers to familiarize yourself with the manner in which tests of controls and substantive tests of transactions are designed.

> **NOTE:** In column three on workpaper 12-1, Bill has written one test of control for each control listed in column two. Notice that each test of control shown in column three relates to a specific existing control in column two.
>
> On workpaper 12-2, Bill has written substantive tests of transactions to directly test each of the audit objectives for sales. Substantive tests of transactions are used to test for monetary misstatements in the transactions, whereas tests of controls are used to test internal controls.

Complete column three on workpaper 14-1 to design the tests of controls for acquisitions.

Complete column two on workpaper 14-2 to design the substantive tests of acquisitions transactions.

> **NOTE:** Column two on workpaper 14-1 has been completed for you to reduce the time requirements of this assignment.

> **TIP:** For each control in column two on workpaper 14-1, write one test of control in column three that could be used to test the control. Keep in mind that the audit procedures commonly used to test controls are (1) inspection of client documents, (2) observation of client activities and events, (3) inquiry of client personnel, or (4) reperformance.
>
> Use workpapers 12-1 and 12-2 as a guide, if necessary.

Completing the assignment

Make sure you **signed off** on each workpaper you completed in this assignment, using 2/23/2019 as the date.

Group the following items together in the order listed and submit them to your instructor for grading, either in person or online at armonddaltonresources.com (consult your instructor):

- Cover page with your printed name, your signature, and the assignment number.
- Workpapers 10-8, 13-1, 13-3, 13-4, 14-1, and 14-2.
- Answers to discussion questions 1 through 7 (see following four pages) if required by your instructor.

Discussion questions

1. After obtaining an understanding of the client's internal controls, the auditor may choose to test some of the controls. If the results of those tests are satisfactory, the auditor may then rely on those controls. What is the primary reason for relying on controls? What are other potential benefits from testing controls?

    _____

    _____

    _____

    _____

    _____

    _____

    _____

    _____

    _____

    _____

2. On some audits, the auditor may choose not to rely on controls, and no tests of controls are performed. Indicate circumstances in which the auditor would choose not to test controls.

    _____

    _____

    _____

    _____

    _____

    _____

    _____

    _____

    _____

3. What is the purpose of a system walkthrough? What is the effect on the auditor's tests of controls if the results of the walkthrough indicate that the controls have not been implemented effectively by the client?

_____

_____

_____

_____

_____

_____

_____

_____

_____

4. Oceanview Marine Company's internal controls were evaluated using both a flowchart and a questionnaire. Discuss the relative advantages and disadvantages of using each type of control documentation.

_____

_____

_____

_____

_____

_____

_____

_____

_____

_____

_____

5. During the audit, the auditor may discover deficiencies in the client's system of internal control. Some of these deficiencies may be considered *significant deficiencies or material weaknesses* as defined by auditing standards. Describe *significant deficiencies* and *material weaknesses* and the auditor's responsibility for communicating them to the client. Do you consider any of the weaknesses in Oceanview's controls over acquisitions to be *significant deficiencies* or *material weaknesses*?

    _____

    _____

    _____

    _____

    _____

    _____

    _____

    _____

    _____

6. A company's management and its independent auditor both have responsibilities related to the company's system of internal control. In the context of the audit of a **private** company, discuss (1) management's responsibilities related to internal controls and (2) the auditor's responsibilities related to internal controls.

    _____

    _____

    _____

    _____

    _____

    _____

    _____

    _____

    _____

7. COSO's *Internal Control—Integrated Framework* is used by many companies as a tool to design and improve their internal control systems. COSO also issued *Enterprise Risk Management – Integrated Framework,* which extends the *Internal Control—Integrated Framework* to the more encompassing topic of enterprise risk management (see https://www.coso. org/Publications/ERM/COSO_ERM_ExecutiveSummary.pdf). Compare and contrast these two frameworks by discussing (1) the components they have in common, and (2) the components added to the *Enterprise Risk Management – Integrated Framework* that are not part of the *Internal Control—Integrated Framework.*

_____

_____

_____

_____

_____

_____

_____

_____

_____

_____

Assignment 5: Perform tests of controls and substantive tests of transactions

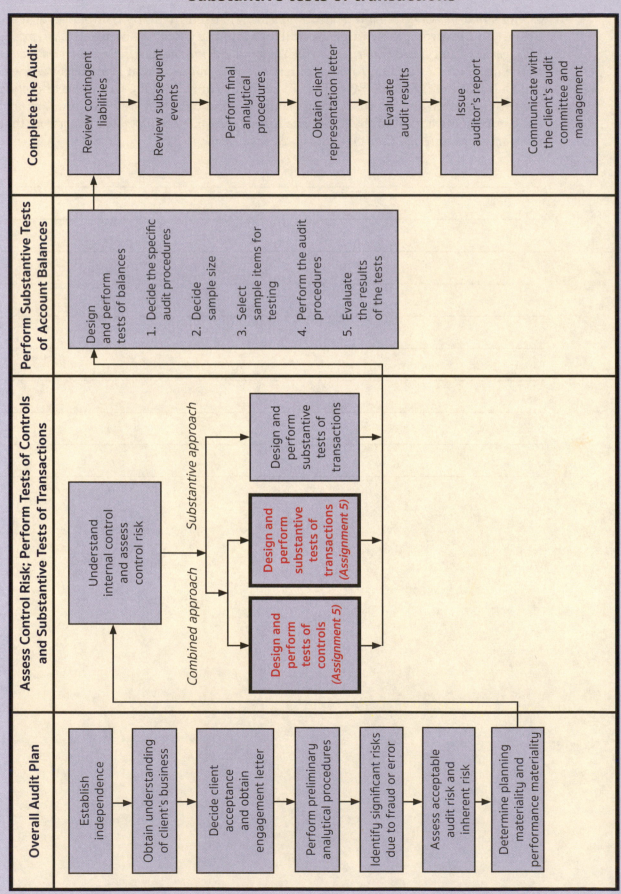

Complete the Audit

- Review contingent liabilities
- Review subsequent events
- Perform final analytical procedures
- Obtain client representation letter
- Evaluate audit results
- Issue auditor's report
- Communicate with the client's audit committee and management

Perform Substantive Tests of Account Balances

Design and perform tests of balances
1. Decide the specific audit procedures
2. Decide sample size
3. Select sample items for testing
4. Perform the audit procedures
5. Evaluate the results of the tests

Assess Control Risk; Perform Tests of Controls and Substantive Tests of Transactions

Understand internal control and assess control risk

Substantive approach

Design and perform substantive tests of transactions

Combined approach

Design and perform substantive tests of transactions *(Assignment 5)*

Design and perform tests of controls *(Assignment 5)*

Overall Audit Plan

- Establish independence
- Obtain understanding of client's business
- Decide client acceptance and obtain engagement letter
- Perform preliminary analytical procedures
- Identify significant risks due to fraud or error
- Assess acceptable audit risk and inherent risk
- Determine planning materiality and performance materiality

ASSIGNMENT 5: Perform tests of controls and substantive tests of transactions

Overview

In this assignment you will:

- ⚓ review and evaluate the results of tests of controls and substantive tests of transactions performed by Bill Cullen for sales.

- ⚓ perform and evaluate tests of controls and substantive tests of transactions for acquisitions.

Auditing concepts

Rearrange the "planning format" audit programs into "performance format" audit programs

In Assignment 4, you designed tests of controls and substantive tests of transactions by preparing a "planning format" audit program (workpapers 14-1 and 14-2). Prior to performing the tests, the planning format audit program must be converted to a "performance format" audit program. This involves rearranging the audit procedures so that they are performed in the most efficient order possible. The auditor will not add or delete procedures or change the wording of the audit procedures during the conversion from the planning format to the performance format. The primary objectives of rearranging the audit program from a planning format to a performance format are:

- combine tests of controls and substantive tests of transactions to provide greater efficiency.
- eliminate duplicate procedures.
- perform all procedures on a given document at one time.
- perform all audit procedures in the most efficient order. For example, by footing a journal and reviewing the journal for unusual items first, the auditor gains a better perspective for performing subsequent tests.

Decide the sample size for tests of controls and substantive tests of transactions

Before deciding the sample size, the auditor must first determine if sampling is practical. There is no need to determine sample size if sampling is not practical. An example of a practical sampling situation is the examination of supporting documents for cash disbursements transactions. An example of a situation where sampling is not practical is deciding whether or not there is adequate separation of duties.

For situations in which sampling is practical, several factors influence the sample size, including:

- *Tolerable Exception Rate (TER)*. TER is the highest exception rate the auditor will permit in the population and still be willing to keep assessed control risk at the level originally planned. For important and highly effective controls (lower control risk), TER is typically between 2% and 7%. For unimportant or low effectiveness controls (higher control risk), TER can be 10% or higher. TER can vary for different attributes. As TER decreases, planned sample sizes will increase. TER is sometimes referred to as the "tolerable deviation rate" or "tolerable rate of occurrence."

- *Expected Population Exception Rate (EPER)*. EPER is the exception rate (deviation rate) the auditor expects to find. When auditing effective internal control systems, EPER is likely to be 0 or 1%. For ineffective systems, it might be as high as 7% or 8%. EPER can vary for different attributes. As EPER increases, planned sample sizes will also increase. EPER is sometimes referred to as the "expected population deviation rate."

- *Acceptable Risk of Overreliance (ARO)*. ARO is the risk the auditor is willing to take of relying on a control when the true population exception rate is **greater** than the auditor's tolerable exception rate (TER). In other words, ARO is the risk of incorrectly relying on a control that is, in fact, **not** operating reliably. In most cases, ARO is set between 5% and 10%, inclusive. As ARO decreases, planned sample sizes will increase.

After the sample size is determined, the auditor must select the sample items from the population for testing. When using nonstatistical sampling, the sample can be selected either judgmentally or randomly. When using statistical sampling, however, the sample must be selected randomly. Most auditors use audit software or spreadsheet programs to select and document random samples.

Perform the tests

The most time-consuming part of tests of controls and substantive tests of transactions is actually performing the tests. The primary step auditors perform when testing transactions is examining documents and related records. An essential part of performing the tests is the documentation of every exception found in the sample. It is also necessary to document the sample size for each attribute tested and the total number of exceptions found. In addition to documenting the sample size, the auditor must specifically identify which transactions were examined. A reader of the workpapers should be able to re-perform the *same* test and achieve the *same* results.

Evaluate the results

There are three steps to evaluating the results of tests of controls or substantive tests of transactions:

1. **Generalize to the population**

   The auditor is interested in the effectiveness of internal controls and whether transactions are properly recorded for the entire population, not just for those items sampled. The auditor generalizes to the population by computing the upper exception rate for each attribute tested. There are two steps to determining the **computed upper exception rate** (CUER): (1) calculate the sample exception rate and (2) estimate sampling risk. Both of these steps are done for each attribute tested.

The sample exception rate is calculated by dividing the actual number of exceptions found in the sample by the sample size (e.g., two exceptions from a sample of 50 is a sample exception rate of 4%).

Sampling risk is the risk that the auditor's sample will lead him/her to an erroneous conclusion; that is, a conclusion that is different from the conclusion that would have been reached had the auditor tested the entire population. The most important determinant of sampling risk is sample size, but acceptable risk of overreliance (ARO) and the actual number of exceptions also affect sampling risk. Smaller sample sizes, more exceptions, and smaller AROs all increase sampling risk.

When using **statistical** sampling, the **computed upper exception rate** (CUER) is determined by using attribute sampling tables which incorporate an appropriate allowance for sampling risk.

When using **nonstatistical** sampling, one way to calculate CUER is to sum the sample exception rate and an estimated allowance for sampling risk. This is the approach followed in this assignment. For example, if the sample exception rate is 1% and the estimated sampling risk is 4%, then CUER is 5%. Other nonstatistical evaluation methods might not include a numerical amount for sampling risk, but sampling risk should be considered by the auditor nevertheless.

2. **Reach conclusions about the effectiveness of internal control and the accounting system**

    To determine whether the internal control or accounting system is operating effectively, the auditor must compare the computed upper exception rate (CUER) to the tolerable exception rate (TER) for each attribute. If CUER exceeds TER, the likely conclusion is that the control or accounting system is less effective than originally thought. When CUER exceeds TER, the most likely action is to increase the assessed level of control risk for one or more objectives, and increase related substantive tests. In contrast, if CUER is less than or equal to TER, the auditor will likely decide that internal controls were operating effectively during the period under audit, which supports an assessment of control risk at less than the maximum level (100%) for one or more objectives.

3. **Analyze exceptions that were found**

    Regardless of whether CUER exceeds TER, the auditor needs to determine the nature and cause of every exception found in the sample. Normally, if CUER is less than or equal to TER, it is unnecessary to expand the related substantive tests beyond those originally planned.

★ CUER > TER; less effective increase assessed level & substantive tests

Requirements

a. In preparation for this assignment, obtain the following from the *Current Workpapers:* 12-6, 14-3, 14-4, 14-7, and 14-8.

These workpapers will be completed in this assignment and turned in to your instructor for grading. Remember to **sign off** on each workpaper as you complete it. Use 2/23/2019 as the completion date for each workpaper you complete in this assignment.

> **ELECTRONIC WORKPAPER OPTION:** In this assignment, you can use Excel to complete and print workpapers 14-7 and 14-8. **These workpapers are included in the file named "Assign 5 Excel_7ed.xlsx."** If you use the Excel versions of those workpapers, you may disregard the copies included in the *Current Workpapers.*
>
> To prevent accidental modifications of his work, Bill has "locked" and "protected" many of the cells in the Excel workpapers. If you need to change any of these locked cells, you will need to first unprotect the workpaper by clicking on REVIEW, UNPROTECT SHEET in the main Excel menu at the top of the screen.

Design tests of controls and substantive tests of transactions

b. On workpapers 12-3 through 12-9, Bill Cullen has nearly completed documenting the results of tests of controls and substantive tests of transactions for sales. Study these workpapers to familiarize yourself with the work already performed by Bill.

c. Bill has not completed the final column on the Statistical Attribute Sampling Data Sheet (workpaper 12-6). Complete this column now by determining the computed upper exception rate (CUER) for each attribute.

> **TIP:** Since Bill used statistical sampling when testing sales transactions, to determine CUER you should use the second attribute sampling table in the Assignment 5 appendix (Assignment 5 ✦ Page 12), along with the information in the Sample Size column and the Number of Exceptions column in the Actual Results section of workpaper 12-6.

For each attribute in column one on workpaper 12-6, compare CUER with TER to determine whether the related internal control has been operating effectively or whether the rate of monetary misstatements is acceptable. On workpaper 12-4, review Bill's conclusions regarding the effectiveness of the internal controls and the accounting system for sales to ensure that they are consistent with your CUER results on workpaper 12-6; change Bill's conclusions if necessary. Sign off on workpaper 12-4, using 2/23/2019 as the date.

Bill has partially completed the audit program for tests of controls and substantive tests of transactions for acquisitions. The audit procedures remaining to be performed have been circled on workpaper 14-3. Follow the steps below to complete these remaining procedures:

Decide sample size

d. On workpaper 14-7, complete the sample size column under Planning.

> **TIP:** Workpaper 14-7 includes descriptions of eight attributes. Testing the eight attributes will satisfy the requirements of steps 1(a) through 1(h) on workpaper 14-3.
>
> Determine the sample size for attributes 1 through 8 using the attribute sampling table in your auditing textbook or the first table provided in the appendix to this assignment. To provide a reference, the sample size for the first attribute has already been entered on workpaper 14-7. You may also use workpaper 12-6 as a guide for completing workpaper 14-7. Keep in mind, however, that workpaper 12-6 uses a statistical approach whereas workpaper 14-7 uses a nonstatistical approach. As a result, the "actual results" sections of these two workpapers differ.

Select the sample items

e. Now, ignoring your answer in step (d) above, assume that the sample size for all eight attributes is **55** items. Complete the sample size column in the Actual Results section on workpaper 14-7 using **55** as the sample size.

Bill has randomly selected 55 purchase voucher packages for testing (see workpaper 14-5). Assume Bill Cullen has performed tests on 50 of the 55 voucher packages and found no exceptions. In step (f) below, you will perform tests of controls and substantive tests of transactions on the remaining five vouchers.

Perform the tests

f. For each of the five vouchers indicated on workpaper 14-8, perform tests of controls and substantive tests of transactions for attributes 1 through 8 listed on workpaper 14-7 using the client documents provided in the *Client Documents* folder.

For each voucher tested, enter an "X" in the appropriate column on workpaper 14-8 to indicate an exception. If a document typically used for the type of transaction you are testing is missing, this will result in an exception for each attribute that requires examination of that document.

TIP: The five vouchers, along with information taken from the voucher register, are summarized on workpaper 14-6.

On workpaper 14-8, the attributes numbers (1 through 8) across the top of the Record of Exceptions matrix refer to the attributes in column one on workpaper 14-7.

On workpaper 14-8, the third to last line on the Record of Exceptions matrix indicates that Bill did not find any exceptions when he tested the other 50 voucher packages.

To test attribute #7, you can identify account classifications based on the chart of accounts in the *Permanent file* (102-1 and 102-2) located near the end of this booklet or the working trial balance in the booklet titled *Current Workpapers* (3-1 to 3-3).

To test attribute #8, compare dates on receiving reports with dates entered in the voucher register (w/p 14-6). If the date on the receiving report is within seven days of the date entered in the voucher register, the acquisition is considered to have been recorded promptly.

NOTE: On workpaper 14-7, you are testing transactions in the acquisitions journal (voucher register) for the **occurrence (existence), accuracy, classification, and timing** objectives. The **completeness** objective must be tested separately, as must the **posting and summarization** objective.

The direction in which you test the **occurrence** and **completeness** objectives is critical to the effectiveness of your tests. When testing **occurrence**, you must begin by selecting a sample of transactions *from the journal* and then vouch them back *to the supporting documents* (receiving reports) to ensure all acquisitions recorded in the journal have been received [see step 1(b) on workpaper 14-3].

In contrast, when testing the **completeness** objective, you test in the opposite direction; i.e., you begin by selecting a *sample of receiving reports* and then trace them *to the journal* to ensure that all acquisitions have been recorded in the journal [see step 2(a) on workpaper 14-3, and workpaper 14-10].

Posting and summarization is usually tested on a block of transactions, rather than a sample of individual transactions, as described in step 4 on workpaper 14-9.

Evaluate the results

g. Complete the rows for the Total Number of Exceptions and Total Sample Size on the bottom of workpaper 14-8.

Using the information on the bottom of workpaper 14-8, complete the remaining columns in workpaper 14-7.

> **TIP:** You might want to re-read pages 3 and 4 in this assignment if you are unsure how to calculate CUER. Remember that you are using nonstatistical sampling.

h. Complete workpaper 14-4. Use workpaper 12-4 as a guide, if necessary. Keep in mind that Bill tested 50 vouchers in addition to those you tested.

When completed, transfer your recommendations from the bottom of workpaper 14-4 to the draft of the management letter (workpaper 93-2, which you began working on in Assignment 2).

> **TIP:** Before writing your conclusion on workpaper 14-4, you might want to re-read the section titled *"Reach conclusions about the effectiveness of internal control and the accounting system"* on page 4 of this assignment. You should state whether, based on the results of the tests performed on workpaper 14-3, control risk for any of the internal control objectives should be increased. You should also indicate the effect of the test results on substantive testing.
>
> For your recommendations in number 3, briefly summarize any suggestions you might make to the client for improving specific controls or aspects of the accounting system.

> **NOTE:** Although not required in this assignment, whenever you find monetary misstatements in the client's accounting records, you will want to bring them to the client's attention so they can be corrected. The auditor does not normally propose adjustments for misstatements detected when performing tests of transactions, unless the misstatements are individually material and have not been previously corrected by the client.

Completing the assignment

Make sure you signed off on the following workpapers completed in this assignment, using 2/23/2019 as the date: 12-6, 14-3, 14-4, 14-7, and 14-8.

Also make sure you **signed off** on each sub-step in step 1 on workpaper 14-3 by writing your initials in the "INIT" columns.

Group the following items together in the order listed and submit them to your instructor for grading, either in person or online at armonddaltonresources.com (consult your instructor):

*   Cover page with your printed name, your signature, and the assignment number.
*   Workpapers 12-6, 14-3, 14-4, 14-7, 14-8, and 93-2.
*   Answers to discussion questions 1 through 4 (see next three pages) if required by your instructor.

Discussion questions

1. For this assignment, the expected population exception rate (EPER) was specified as 1% or 2%, the tolerable exception rate (TER) was specified as 7% or 8%, and the acceptable risk of overreliance (ARO) was specified as 10% for all attributes in the audit of acquisitions transactions. Indicate how each of these variables (EPER, TER, and ARO) should be determined. What is the effect on sample size of lowering each variable (EPER, TER, and ARO)?

_____

_____

_____

_____

_____

_____

_____

_____

_____

_____

_____

_____

2. When the computed upper exception rate (CUER) exceeds the tolerable exception rate (TER), the auditor will likely increase the assessed level of control risk and increase one or more related substantive tests. What other courses of action are available to the auditor when CUER exceeds TER?

_____

_____

_____

_____

_____

_____

3. The study and evaluation of internal controls in Assignment 4 identified deficiencies in internal controls over acquisitions. Did any of these deficiencies result in misstatements in the recording of transactions? Explain why deficiencies in internal controls might not always result in significant misstatements when transactions are recorded.

_____

_____

_____

_____

_____

_____

_____

_____

_____

4. You performed tests of controls and substantive tests of transactions for acquisitions using nonstatistical sampling. The tests of controls and substantive tests of transactions for sales transactions were performed using statistical sampling. Indicate the significant differences in these approaches in planning the sample, performing the audit procedures, and evaluating the results of the sample.

_____

_____

_____

_____

_____

_____

_____

_____

_____

_____

_____

_____

ASSIGNMENT 5: Appendix

ATTRIBUTE SAMPLING TABLES*

Determining the Sample Size 10% Acceptable Risk of Overreliance									
Expected Exception Rate	Tolerable Exception Rate (In Percentage)								
	2	3	4	5	6	7	8	9	10
.00	114	76	57	45	38	32	28	25	22
.50	194	129	96	77	64	55	48	42	38
1.00	—	176	96	77	64	55	48	42	38
1.50	—	—	132	105	64	55	48	42	38
2.00	—	—	198	132	88	75	48	42	38
2.50	—	—	—	158	110	75	65	58	38
3.00	—	—	—	—	132	94	65	58	52

Determining the Computer Upper Exception Rate (CUER) 10% Acceptable Risk of Overreliance								
Sample Size	Actual Number of Exceptions							
	0	1	2	3	4	5	6	7
25	8.8	14.7	20.0	—	—	—	—	—
30	7.4	12.4	16.8	—	—	—	—	—
40	5.6	9.4	12.8	16.0	19.0	—	—	—
50	4.6	7.6	10.3	12.9	15.4	17.8	—	—
55	4.2	6.9	9.4	11.8	14.1	16.3	18.4	—
60	3.8	6.4	8.7	10.8	12.9	15.0	16.9	18.9
70	3.3	5.5	7.5	9.3	11.1	12.9	14.6	16.3
90	2.6	4.3	5.9	7.3	8.7	10.1	11.5	12.8
100	2.3	3.9	5.3	6.6	7.9	9.1	10.3	11.5
125	1.9	3.1	4.3	5.3	6.3	7.3	8.3	9.3
150	1.6	2.6	3.6	4.4	5.3	6.1	7.0	7.8
200	1.2	2.0	2.7	3.4	4.0	4.6	5.3	5.9

* Source: Tables are partial excerpts from the AICPA (2017) *Audit Sampling* Audit Guide.

Assignment 6: Perform audit of accounts receivable

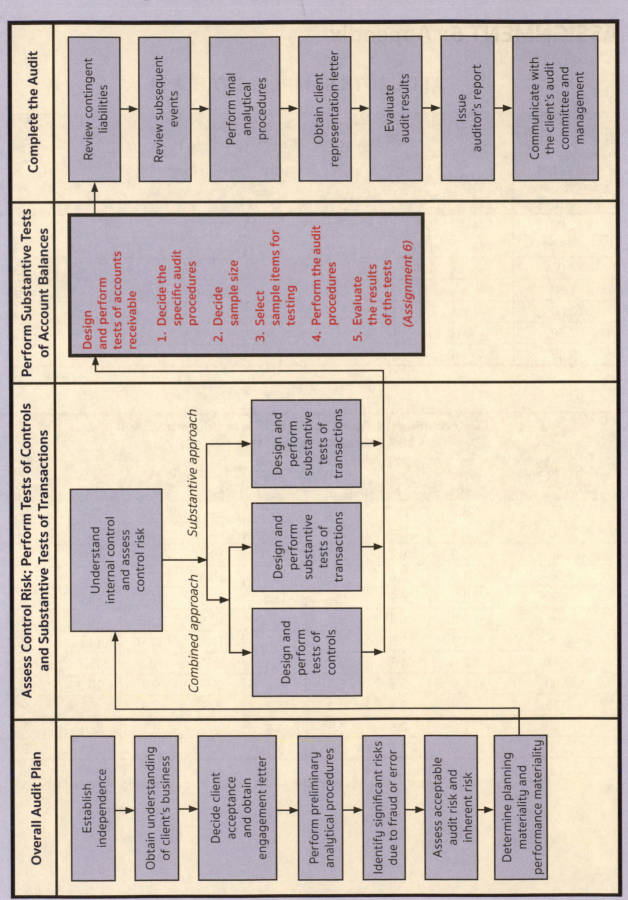

Complete the Audit

- Review contingent liabilities
- Review subsequent events
- Perform final analytical procedures
- Obtain client representation letter
- Evaluate audit results
- Issue auditor's report
- Communicate with the client's audit committee and management

Perform Substantive Tests of Account Balances

Design and perform tests of accounts receivable

1. Decide the specific audit procedures
2. Decide sample size
3. Select sample items for testing
4. Perform the audit procedures
5. Evaluate the results of the tests *(Assignment 6)*

Assess Control Risk; Perform Tests of Controls and Substantive Tests of Transactions

Understand internal control and assess control risk

Substantive approach

Design and perform substantive tests of transactions

Combined approach

- Design and perform tests of controls
- Design and perform substantive tests of transactions

Overall Audit Plan

- Establish independence
- Obtain understanding of client's business
- Decide client acceptance and obtain engagement letter
- Perform preliminary analytical procedures
- Identify significant risks due to fraud or error
- Assess acceptable audit risk and inherent risk
- Determine planning materiality and performance materiality

ASSIGNMENT 6: Perform audit of accounts receivable

Overview

In this assignment you will audit Oceanview Marine Company's accounts receivable balance.

There are five closely related steps in the audit of accounts receivable:

1. Decide the specific audit procedures to be performed for each audit objective.
2. Decide the sample size for each audit procedure.
3. Select sample items for testing.
4. Perform the audit procedures.
5. Evaluate the results of the tests and conclude whether the accounts receivable balance is fairly stated.

> **NOTE:** Sampling is an essential element of the testing of accounts receivable. This assignment allows you to complete the testing of accounts receivable using any of three acceptable sampling methods based on the AICPA (2017) *Audit Sampling* Audit Guide.
>
> 1. **Option A** — Nonstatistical sampling
> 2. **Option B** — Monetary unit sampling
> 3. **Option C** — Difference estimation
>
> You should use one of these methods as indicated by your instructor. If your instructor does not suggest a method, use the first option involving the use of nonstatistical sampling.

Auditing concepts

Nature of the audit of accounts receivable

The audit of the year-end accounts receivable balance involves accumulating sufficient appropriate evidence to evaluate whether accounts receivable balances are fairly stated and properly disclosed in the financial statements. In addition to testing whether the gross amount of accounts receivable is fairly stated, the auditor must determine whether accounts receivable is stated at net realizable value by testing the adequacy of the allowance for doubtful accounts. One of the primary procedures performed to determine whether gross amounts of accounts receivable are fairly stated is the confirmation of a sample of accounts receivable balances.

Confirmation of accounts receivable

Confirmations are considered highly reliable evidence because they originate with a third party. Confirmation of accounts receivable is generally required by U.S auditing standards, unless:

- the auditor considers external confirmations to provide ineffective evidence because response rates are inadequate or responses are unreliable.
- the combined level of inherent risk and control risk is low, and the other planned substantive procedures provide sufficient evidence.

It is desirable to confirm year-end balances, but confirmations are often sent one or two months prior to year-end to facilitate timely completion of the audit. In this assignment, it is assumed that confirmations were sent at year-end.

If a response to the confirmation request is not received, the auditor will perform alternative procedures to verify the balance. Common alternative procedures include agreeing the receivable balance to subsequent payment, or vouching the receivable balance to supporting invoices and shipping documents.

Statistical and nonstatistical sampling

Auditors generally do not test all transactions or balances that make up an account. Auditing standards provide guidance to auditors when audit tests are based on a sample from a population. Misstatements detected in the sample should be projected to the population, and adequate consideration should be given to sampling risk. Both statistical and nonstatistical sampling methods are allowed, and auditing standards do not explicitly endorse one method over the other.

The two primary differences between statistical and nonstatistical sampling are (1) the sample selection method, and (2) measurement of sampling risk. When using nonstatistical sampling, the auditor may select sample items non-randomly (judgmentally), systematically (with a non-random start), or randomly. However, when the auditor chooses to employ statistical sampling, sample items must be selected randomly, using either a purely random selection method, or a systematic selection method with a random start. The measurement of sampling risk is performed judgmentally when using nonstatistical sampling, while it is done mathematically for statistical sampling.

Both methods of sampling have their own advantages. Statistical sampling can (1) help the auditor determine an efficient sample size, and (2) quantify sampling risk. On the other hand, nonstatistical sampling is less complex and less time-consuming than statistical sampling. Both statistical and nonstatistical sampling methods are acceptable and used in practice.

Sampling for tests of balances

Sampling methods involve the following five general steps:

1. **Plan the sample**

   Audit procedures are designed for each audit objective (i.e., existence, completeness, accuracy, cutoff, and so on). Testing the existence of accounts receivable is the most important audit objective for accounts receivable, although several other objectives are also important. The most important audit procedure for accounts receivable is confirmation of accounts receivable. Confirmation of receivables helps satisfy the *existence, accuracy,* and *cutoff* objectives.

While sampling is usually appropriate when confirming accounts receivable, sampling is not possible when performing procedures such as footing the aged listing of accounts receivable and tracing the total to the general ledger. Thus, the auditor needs to determine whether sampling is practical for the audit procedures to be performed.

2. **Determine sample size**

In situations where sampling can be used, the auditor must determine the appropriate extent of tests of balances for each audit objective for accounts receivable. Several factors influence the appropriate extent of testing (i.e., sample size). These factors include:

- *Tolerable misstatement*—tolerable misstatement is performance materiality applied to an individual sampling application. It is inversely related to sample size (the smaller the tolerable misstatement, the larger the sample will be).
- *Book value of the recorded population*—directly related to sample size (the larger the account's year-end balance, the larger the sample will be).
- *Expected misstatement in the population*—directly related to sample size (the larger the expected misstatement in the population, the larger the sample needs to be).
- *Acceptable risk of incorrect acceptance (ARIA)*—inversely related to sample size (the smaller the auditor's acceptable risk of incorrect acceptance, the larger the sample will be). ARIA depends on audit risk model assessments and the results of other substantive tests, such as analytical procedures and substantive tests of transactions.

Formulas are often used to determine the appropriate sample size for various sampling methods. Such formulas generally take into consideration each of the above factors, although the actual factors determining sample size will depend upon the sampling method used.

3. **Select sample items for testing**

When using statistical sampling methods such as monetary unit sampling or difference estimation, sample items *must* be selected randomly. Judgmental selection is permissible with nonstatistical testing, but random selection is recommended. One method of random selection is to use a spreadsheet program or audit software to generate a list of random numbers. Systematic selection with a random start is another method and is used in this assignment.

The sample items selected depend upon the testing method used. The sampling unit in monetary unit sampling is individual dollars in accounts receivable, and the sampling unit in difference estimation is individual customer accounts. Auditors may stratify the population (account balance) into sub-populations, performing extensive testing on some of the sub-populations, and less testing on other sub-populations. For instance, the emphasis on overstatements more than understatements in the audit of accounts receivable motivates auditors to concentrate on certain items more than others. In the confirmation of accounts receivable, auditors emphasize customer accounts with large balances.

4. **Perform the audit procedures**

The most time-consuming part of auditing accounts receivable or any other account is performing the tests, such as examining confirmation responses.

An important part of performing the tests is reconciling differences between the client's recorded amounts and amounts supported by the auditor's evidence. For example, suppose a customer disagrees with the amount shown on the confirmation request. The auditor must determine whether the difference is a client misstatement, timing difference, or customer misstatement. The auditor ordinarily reconciles the recorded amount and the confirmation by first requesting that the client investigate the difference. The auditor then examines supporting documentation or other evidence to support the client's conclusions and to determine the amount of the misstatement, if any.

5. **Evaluate the results of the tests and conclude whether accounts receivable is fairly stated**

When the auditor evaluates the results of the tests for an account such as accounts receivable, the primary objective is to decide whether the account is materially misstated. The auditor must also decide whether prior assessments of control risk and inherent risk require revision based on the findings in the tests of the account balance.

a. **Generalize to the population.** The auditor is primarily interested in an estimate of the misstatements in the account balance, not just the misstatements found in the sample. The sample misstatements are projected to the population to estimate the misstatements in the account balance. The auditor should also give appropriate consideration to sampling risk, even when nonstatistical methods are used.

b. **Compare computed misstatement bounds to tolerable misstatement and decide acceptability of the recorded account balance.** The auditor must compare the computed misstatement bounds to tolerable misstatement to determine if the account balance is fairly stated. There are several possible actions:

   - *Accept the population as stated*. This conclusion is likely if the computed misstatement bounds are within tolerable misstatement.
   - *Request the client to adjust the population*. Auditors should always inform their clients of any misstatements found in an account balance. If the computed misstatement bounds exceed tolerable misstatement, then an adjusting journal entry to correct the misstatements *may* reduce projected misstatement sufficiently to make the account acceptable.
   - *Expand audit tests*. If neither of the first two options applies, the auditor may expand substantive tests of balances, either by increasing the sample size or performing other tests. It is typically not efficient to test more items if the auditor expects to find the same rate of misstatement in the additional items tested as was found in the original items tested. In this case, performing other tests of the accounts receivable balance may be necessary.
   - *Request that the client re-work the population*. In rare cases, the client may need to determine the account balance again. If this is necessary, the auditor will need to re-audit the population.

---

c. **Analyze misstatements and reassess risks.** Regardless of whether the auditor accepts or rejects the recorded account balance, the auditor should analyze the nature and cause of every misstatement found in the sample. Normally, if the misstatement bounds are less than or equal to tolerable misstatement, it is unnecessary to expand the audit tests beyond those originally planned. However, the auditor may decide that the original assessment of control risk or inherent risk may require revision, given the new information.

Option A: Audit of accounts receivable using nonstatistical sampling

Requirements

a. In preparation for this assignment, obtain the following from the *Current Workpapers*: 21-1 through 21-3, 21-5, 21-6, and 21-17 through 21-21.

These workpapers will be completed in this assignment and submitted to your instructor for grading. Remember to **sign off** on each workpaper as you complete it. Use 2/24/2019 as the completion date for each workpaper you complete in this assignment.

> **ELECTRONIC WORKPAPER OPTION:** In this assignment, you can complete and print workpapers 21-1, 21-2, 21-6, and 21-17 through 21-21 using Microsoft Excel. **These workpapers are included in the file named "Assign 6 Option A Excel_7ed.xlsx."** You may disregard the copies of these workpapers in the *Current Workpapers*.
>
> To prevent accidental modifications of the Excel file, each sheet has been "protected." If you need to make changes to a sheet, you will need to first unprotect the sheet by clicking on REVIEW, UNPROTECT SHEET.

> **NOTE:** On workpaper 21-1, notice that Bill has agreed the figures for accounts receivable and the allowance for doubtful accounts to the general ledger. Bill has also agreed both amounts for 2017 to the prior year's workpaper file.

Plan the sample

b. Specific audit procedures for accounts receivable have been designed by your firm and form the *Audit Program for Accounts Receivable* on workpapers 21-3 through 21-5. Before continuing, carefully read the audit program to be sure that you understand the purpose of each audit procedure, including those procedures already completed by Bill Cullen.

Also study the work completed by Bill on workpapers 21-7 through 21-16.

c. Complete step 1 on the audit program (workpaper 21-3).

> **TIP:** *The Planned Tests of Balances Matrix* mentioned in step 1 is found on workpaper 21-6. Bill has completed the first three rows for you.

> **NOTE:** The *Planned Tests of Balances Matrix* summarizes the factors that influence the extent of tests of balances for accounts receivable.
>
> The first factor, acceptable audit risk, is *inversely* related to the extent of testing; i.e., as acceptable audit risk increases, the extent of testing decreases.
>
> Each of the other factors is *directly* related to the extent of testing; e.g., as inherent risk or control risk increases, the extent of testing increases.
>
> Notice that each factor is evaluated separately for each audit objective.

Decide sample size for confirmation of accounts receivable

d. Use workpaper 21-17, along with the following information, to determine an appropriate sample size for the confirmation of receivables.

All individually material customer accounts greater than tolerable misstatement are usually selected for testing. There are 13 customer accounts greater than tolerable misstatement of $40,000; the combined dollar value of these accounts is $1,166,116. A sample of the remaining accounts (accounts less than, or equal to, $40,000) is also selected for testing.

The random sample of the customer accounts will be selected based on the following formula:

$$\text{Sample Size} = \frac{\text{Population Recorded Amount} \times \text{Confidence Factor}}{\text{Tolerable Misstatement}}$$

Risk of Incorrect Acceptance	Confidence of Sample	Confidence Factor
37%	63%	1
14%	86%	2
5%	95%	3

The population recorded amount is the book value of the population less the individually material amounts greater than tolerable misstatement of $40,000, totaling $1,166,116.

ADDITIONAL INFORMATION: Since (1) inherent risks for the existence and accuracy objectives are medium (see workpaper 21-6), and (2) the results of tests of controls and substantive tests of transactions for the sales cycle were generally favorable, the combined assessment of inherent and control risk is moderate. The results of substantive tests of transactions and analytical procedures were generally favorable. Based on these factors, a confidence factor of 2 was used, corresponding to a risk of incorrect acceptance of 14%. Information regarding the selection of the appropriate confidence factor is already indicated on workpaper 21-17. Assume tolerable misstatement for accounts receivable is $40,000.

ELECTRONIC WORKPAPER OPTION: In cell B20 on workpaper 21-17, Bill has entered a formula to determine the sample size. You should verify that the formula is correct; make corrections if necessary.

Select sample items for testing

e. Independent of your answer in requirement (d), assume your sample size consists of the following:

- All 13 customer accounts greater than tolerable misstatement.
- A random sample of 35 of the remaining 73 customer accounts.

Using the year-end accounts receivable listing (workpapers 21-7 through 21-9), select the first five customer accounts from each part of the sample to be confirmed. Use workpaper 21-18 to document your selections.

ELECTRONIC WORKPAPER OPTION: Complete and print workpaper 21-18 using Excel.

TIP: In selecting the sample of amounts less than tolerable misstatement, begin by calculating the sampling interval in the space provided on 21-18. The first account for each sample group and the random starting point (1st account) for the sample have been selected for you. To reduce the time demands, you are only required to select the next four items for each part of the sample.

NOTE: In this assignment, systematic selection with a random start is used to select accounts for testing. There are many other methods of selection that would be acceptable in practice. The sampling interval is usually larger for companies with a large number of customers.

Perform the audit procedures

f. Assume that you mailed 48 confirmations and all have been returned to you from the customers. Five of the 48 customers disagreed with the client regarding the amount owed (see workpapers 21-10 through 21-14). Bill Cullen investigated the differences and wrote explanations on each of these five confirmations. After reading Bill's comments, decide whether the differences are client misstatements and should be projected to the population, or whether they are customer misstatements or timing differences that can be disregarded. Document your decisions by completing workpaper 21-19.

> **ELECTRONIC WORKPAPER OPTION:** Complete and print workpaper 21-19 using Excel.

> **TIPS:** When completing workpaper 21-19, be sure to list each difference in the appropriate section. Recall that the first group of accounts selected for testing consists of all accounts whose book value exceeds $40,000, while a sample was selected of accounts whose book value is equal to, or less than, $40,000.
>
> When calculating the net misstatement on workpaper 21-19, overstatements should be treated as positive numbers and understatements as negative numbers

Evaluate the results of the tests and conclude whether accounts receivable is fairly stated

g. Complete workpaper 21-20 to project misstatements to the population and calculate the allowance for sampling risk.

Complete the first three of the four sections on workpaper 21-21 to document your decision regarding the acceptability of the account balance. You might want to re-read page 5 of this assignment before completing this workpaper. In the Conclusion section, indicate whether, in your opinion, accounts receivable is fairly stated or whether further testing will be necessary based on the results of your confirmations of accounts receivable.

> **ELECTRONIC WORKPAPER OPTION:** Complete and print workpapers 21-20 and 21-21 using Excel. Follow these steps:
>
> 1. On workpaper 21-20, verify that the net misstatement for amounts greater than tolerable misstatement has been transferred correctly from workpaper 21-19. Also verify that the projected misstatement for the sample of items below tolerable misstatement has been calculated correctly using the formula provided on workpaper 21-20. Make any necessary corrections to the formulas.
>
> 2. Verify that the allowance for sampling risk has been calculated correctly on workpaper 21-20. Make any necessary corrections to the formulas.

h. Complete the bottom section of workpaper 21-21. Refer to the Assignment 6 appendix (Assignment SIX ✦ Page 29) for firm policy regarding the evaluation and disposition of actual and projected misstatements identified during audit testing, including description of the audit misstatement posting threshold. The posting threshold has been set at $2,000 for the Oceanview audit. Misstatements, including projected misstatements, below this amount are considered trivial and do not need to be accumulated. Amounts greater than the audit misstatement threshold should be included on the summary of uncorrected misstatements to determine if the aggregate amount of unadjusted misstatements is material. The projected misstatement should be reduced by the amount of adjusting entries, if any, to accounts receivable (do not include the adjusting journal entry to the allowance for doubtful accounts prepared by Bill Cullen).

Carry forward any unadjusted projected misstatement greater than the posting threshold to the *Summary of Uncorrected Misstatements* (workpaper 90-1).

> **TIP:** The Identified Misstatement column on workpaper 90-1 includes the amount of any misstatements identified in your testing on workpaper 21-19 that have not been adjusted by the client. Your remaining *unadjusted projected misstatement* on workpaper 21-21 should be entered in the Likely Aggregate Misstatement, Current Assets, and Income Before Taxes columns on workpaper 90-1.
>
> At the conclusion of the audit, the *Summary of Uncorrected Misstatements* will be reviewed and compared to materiality to decide if further adjusting entries are required to reduce the misstatements to an acceptable level.

i. Assume the client agrees with the adjusting journal entry(ies) proposed on workpaper 21-2.

- Write the net effect (on accounts receivable and the allowance for doubtful accounts) of the entry(ies) in the Net Adjustments column on the accounts receivable leadsheet (workpaper 21-1), and write the new account balance in the 2018 Adjusted Balance column on the leadsheet. Note that Bill has already posted the adjustment to the allowance for doubtful accounts and cross-referenced the balance to workpaper 21-15. You should complete the extensions on the leadsheet, and cross-reference the balance for Account 1100 – accounts receivable. The entry(ies), including the effect on accounts other than accounts receivable, will be posted to the trial balance in Assignment 10.

> **ELECTRONIC WORKPAPER OPTION:** Complete and print workpapers 21-1 and 21-2 using Excel.

Complete the conclusion section, step 22, on workpaper 21-5.

Completing the assignment

Make sure you **signed off** on the following workpapers completed in this assignment, using 2/24/2019 as the date: 21-1 through 21-3, 21-5, 21-6, and 21-17 through 21-21.

Also make sure you **signed off** on step 1 on workpaper 21-3 by writing your initials in the INIT column, and added a reference to workpaper 21-6 in the W/P column.

Also make sure you **signed off** on steps 3a, 3b, 3c, and 3d on workpaper 21-3, added references to the appropriate workpapers in the W/P column, and added any necessary explanations in the COMMENTS column.

Group the following items together in the order listed and submit them to your instructor for grading, either in person or online at armonddaltonresources.com (consult your instructor):

- Cover page with your printed name, your signature, and the assignment number.
- Workpapers 21-1 through 21-3, 21-5, 21-6, and 21-17 through 21-21.
- Answers to discussion questions 1 through 6 (Assignment SIX + Pages 26 through 28) if required by your instructor.

OPTION B: Audit of accounts receivable using monetary unit sampling

Requirements

a. In preparation for this assignment, obtain the following from the *Current Workpapers*: 21-1 through 21-3, 21-5, 21-6, and 21-22 through 21-26.

These workpapers will be completed in this assignment and submitted to your instructor for grading. Remember to **sign off** on each workpaper as you complete it. Use 2/24/2019 as the completion date for each workpaper you complete in this assignment.

> **ELECTRONIC WORKPAPER OPTION:** In this assignment, you can complete and print workpapers 21-1, 21-2, 21-6, and 21-22 through 21-26 using Microsoft Excel. **These workpapers are included in the file named "Assign 6 Option B Excel_7ed.xlsx."** You may disregard the copies of these workpapers included in the *Current Workpapers*.
>
> To prevent accidental modifications of the Excel file, each sheet has been "protected." If you need to make changes to a sheet, you will need to first unprotect the sheet by clicking REVIEW, UNPROTECT SHEET.

> **NOTE:** On workpaper 21-1, notice that Bill has agreed the figures for accounts receivable and the allowance for doubtful accounts to the general ledger. Bill has also agreed both amounts for 2017 to the prior year's workpaper file

Plan the sample

b. Specific audit procedures for accounts receivable have been designed by your firm and form the *Audit Program for Accounts Receivable* on workpapers 21-3 through 21-5. Before continuing, carefully read through the audit program to be sure that you understand the purpose of each audit procedure, including those procedures already completed by Bill Cullen.

Also study the work completed by Bill on workpapers 21-7 through 21-16.

c. Complete step 1 on the audit program (workpaper 21-3).

> **TIP:** The *Planned Tests of Balances Matrix* mentioned in step 1 is found on workpaper 21-6. Bill has completed the first three rows for you.

> **ELECTRONIC WORKPAPER OPTION:** Complete and print workpaper 21-6 in Excel.

NOTE: The *Planned Tests of Balances Matrix* summarizes the factors that influence the extent of tests of balances for accounts receivable.

The first factor, acceptable audit risk, is *inversely* related to the extent of testing; i.e., as acceptable audit risk increases, the extent of testing decreases.

Each of the other factors is *directly* related to the extent of testing; e.g., as inherent risk or control risk increases, the extent of testing increases.

Notice that each factor is evaluated separately for each audit objective.

Decide sample size for confirmation of accounts receivable

d. Use workpaper 21-22, along with the following information, to determine an appropriate sample size for the confirmation of receivables.

ELECTRONIC WORKPAPER OPTION: Complete and print workpaper 21-22 using Excel.

ADDITIONAL INFORMATION: Since (1) inherent risks for the existence and accuracy objectives are medium (see workpaper 21-6), (2) the results of tests of controls and substantive tests of transactions for the sales cycle were generally favorable, and (3) Oceanview's financial condition is strong, assume that your acceptable risk of incorrect acceptance for accounts receivable is 20%.

Also assume your tolerable misstatement for accounts receivable is $40,000 and your estimated (or "expected") misstatement in accounts receivable is $4,000.

Select sample items for testing

e. Independent of your answer in requirement (d), assume your sample size consists of the following:

- All 13 customer accounts greater than tolerable misstatement.
- A monetary unit sample of 35 *dollar units*.

Using the year-end accounts receivable listing (workpapers 21-7 through 21-9), select the first five customer accounts from each part of the sample to be confirmed. Use systematic dollar unit selection to select the sample items for confirmation. Use workpaper 21-23 to document your selections.

ELECTRONIC WORKPAPER OPTION: Complete and print workpaper 21-23 using Excel.

TIPS: Round the sampling interval **downward** to rounded hundred dollars (e.g., $567.89 would be rounded **down** to $500.00).

Use the cumulative total column on workpaper 21-7 to identify the names of the customers whose accounts contain the dollar units selected for testing. (In the Amount Confirmed column on workpaper 21-23, write the customer's total balance, not the cumulative total.)

NOTE: The random starting point ($8,000) and the first sample item have been selected for you. To reduce the time demands, you are required to select the next four sample items instead of all 35 sample items.

Perform the audit procedures

f.   Assume that you mailed 48 confirmations and all have been returned to you from the customers. Five of the 48 customers disagreed with the client regarding the amount owed (see workpapers 21-10 through 21-14). Bill Cullen investigated the differences and wrote explanations on each of these five confirmations. After reading Bill's comments, decide whether the differences are client misstatements and should be projected to the population, or whether they are customer misstatements or timing differences that can be disregarded. Document your decisions by completing the first six columns in workpaper 21-24.

ELECTRONIC WORKPAPER OPTION: Complete and print workpaper 21-24 using Excel.

TIPS: When completing workpaper 21-24, be sure to list each difference in the appropriate section. The first section includes the first group of accounts selected for testing whose book value exceeds $40,000. In addition, the first section includes amounts less than tolerable misstatement, but larger than the sampling interval. These are included with the amounts greater than tolerable misstatement since the misstatements in any account larger than the sampling interval are not projected.

Complete the "tainting" column (column seven) in workpaper 21-24. For differences not involving a client misstatement, write "N/A" in column seven. Round taintings **upward** (never downward) to four decimal places (e.g., 1/3 would be rounded to 0.3334)

When calculating the net misstatement on workpaper 21-24, overstatements should be treated as positive numbers and understatements as negative numbers.

Evaluate the results of the tests and conclude whether accounts receivable is fairly stated

g. Workpapers 21-25 and 21-26 are used to summarize the client misstatements found, to project these misstatements to the population, and to decide the acceptability of the account balance.

Complete workpapers 21-25 and 21-26 using the following steps:

1. On workpaper 21-25, begin by listing the taintings (from workpaper 21-24), ranked from largest to smallest. Also list the corresponding customer names. Next, calculate each projected misstatement by multiplying each tainting by the sampling interval. Add the misstatements found in customers' accounts larger than the sampling interval from the top half of workpaper 21-24 to calculate the total projected misstatement

> **TIP:** Round each projected misstatement to the nearest dollar.

> **TIP:** Misstatements are normally projected to the population by multiplying their tainting by the sampling interval. However, this is true only for misstatements found in customer accounts whose recorded value is *less than* the sampling interval.
>
> Note that the MUS sample was calculated only for amounts less than tolerable misstatement. The entire population of customer accounts whose recorded value exceeds tolerable misstatement was selected for testing (i.e., not sampled). In addition, any remaining customer accounts whose recorded value is equal to, or exceeds, the sampling interval will also always be selected for testing using interval sampling. Thus, there is no need to project misstatements found in accounts whose recorded value equals or exceeds the sampling interval. Rather, the actual amount of the misstatement is used as the projected misstatement.

> **ELECTRONIC WORKPAPER OPTION:** Complete and print workpapers 21-25 and 21-26 using Excel.
>
> Verify that the formulas entered by Bill in column C of workpaper 21-25 are correct (each tainting should be rounded **up** to four decimal places). For differences not involving a client misstatement, enter "N/A" in the tainting column.

2. Calculate the upper limit on misstatements on workpaper 21-25, column 6. First multiply each projected misstatement by the incremental changes in the confidence factor (Bill has already written the appropriate incremental changes in column 5). Add basic precision, which is the sampling interval multiplied by the appropriate confidence factor.

> **ELECTRONIC WORKPAPER OPTION:** Verify that the formulas for the incremental allowance for sampling risk and basic precision as determined by Bill are correct. Make corrections if necessary.

3. Use the top section of workpaper 21-26 to document your decision regarding the acceptability of the account balance. You might want to re-read page 5 of this assignment before completing this workpaper.

> **TIP:** Recall that the tolerable misstatement for accounts receivable is $40,000.

4. On workpaper 21-26, write your conclusions regarding whether accounts receivable is fairly stated or whether further testing will be necessary based on the results of your confirmations of accounts receivable.

h. Complete the bottom section of workpaper 21-26. Refer to the Assignment 6 appendix (Assignment SIX ✦ Page 29) for firm policy regarding the evaluation and disposition of actual and projected misstatements identified during audit testing, including the description of the audit misstatement posting threshold. The posting threshold has been set at $2,000 for the Oceanview audit. Misstatements, including projected misstatements, below this amount are considered trivial and do not need to be accumulated. Amounts greater than the audit misstatement threshold should be included on the *Summary of Uncorrected Misstatements* (workpaper 90-1) to determine if the aggregate amount of unadjusted misstatements is material. The projected misstatement should be reduced by the amount of adjusting entries, if any, to accounts receivable (do not include the adjusting journal entry to the allowance for doubtful accounts prepared by Bill Cullen).

Carry forward any unadjusted projected misstatement greater than the posting threshold to the *Summary of Uncorrected Misstatements* (workpaper 90-1).

> **TIP:** The Identified Misstatement column on workpaper 90-1 includes the amount of any misstatements identified in your testing on workpaper 21-19 that have not been adjusted by the client. Your remaining *unadjusted projected misstatement* on workpaper 21-26 should be entered in the Likely Aggregate Misstatement, Current Assets, and Income Before Taxes columns on workpaper 90-1.

> **NOTE:** Unadjusted actual and projected misstatements are carried forward to the *Summary of Uncorrected Misstatements* (workpaper 90-1).
>
> At the conclusion of the audit, the *Summary of Uncorrected Misstatements* will be reviewed and compared to materiality to decide if further adjusting entries are required to reduce the misstatements to an acceptable level.

i. Assume the client agrees with the adjusting journal entry(ies) proposed on workpaper 21-2.

- Write the net effect (on accounts receivable and the allowance for doubtful accounts) of the entry(ies) in the Net Adjustments column on the accounts receivable leadsheet (workpaper 21-1), and write the new account balance in the 2018 Adjusted Balance column on the leadsheet. You should include the entry already proposed for the allowance for doubtful accounts. Note that Bill has already posted the adjustment to the allowance for doubtful accounts and cross-referenced the balance to workpaper 21-15. You should complete the extensions on the leadsheet, and cross-reference the balance for Account 1100 – accounts receivable. The entry(ies), including the effect on accounts other than accounts receivable, will be posted to the trial balance in Assignment 10.

> **ELECTRONIC WORKPAPER OPTION:** Complete and print workpapers 21-1 and 21-2 using Excel.

k. Complete the conclusion section, step 22, on workpaper 21-5.

Completing the assignment

Make sure you **signed off** on the following workpapers completed in this assignment, using 2/24/2019 as the date: 21-1 through 21-3, 21-5, 21-6, and 21-22 through 21-26.

Also make sure you **signed off** on step 1 on workpaper 21-3 by writing your initials in the INIT column, and added a reference to workpaper 21-6 in the W/P column.

Also make sure you **signed off** on steps 3a, 3b, 3c, and 3d on workpaper 21-3, added references to the appropriate workpapers in the W/P column, and added any necessary explanations in the COMMENTS column.

Group the following items together in the order listed and submit them to your instructor for grading, either in person or online at armonddaltonresources.com (consult your instructor):

- Cover page with your printed name, your signature, and the assignment number.
- Workpapers 21-1 through 21-3, 21-5, 21-6, and 21-22 through 21-26.
- Answers to discussion questions 1 through 6 (Assignment SIX ✦ Pages 26 through 28) if required by your instructor.

OPTION C: Audit of accounts receivable using variables sampling based on difference estimation

Requirements

a. In preparation for this assignment, obtain the following from the *Current Workpapers*: 21-1 through 21-3, 21-5, 21-6, and 21-27 through 21-32.

These workpapers will be completed in this assignment and submitted to your instructor for grading. Remember to **sign off** on each workpaper as you complete it. Use 2/24/2019 as the completion date for each workpaper you complete in this assignment.

> **ELECTRONIC WORKPAPER OPTION:** In this assignment, you can complete and print workpapers 21-1, 21-2, 21-6, and 21-27 through 21-32 using Microsoft Excel. **These workpapers are included in the file named "Assign 6 Option C Excel_7ed.xlsx."** You may disregard the copies of these workpapers in the *Current Workpapers*.
>
> To prevent accidental modifications of the Excel file, each sheet has been "protected." If you need to make changes to a sheet, you will need to first unprotect the sheet by clicking REVIEW, UNPROTECT SHEET.

> **NOTE:** On workpaper 21-1, notice that Bill has agreed the figures for accounts receivable and the allowance for doubtful accounts to the general ledger. Bill has also agreed both amounts for 2017 to the prior year's workpapers file.

Plan the sample

b. Specific audit procedures for accounts receivable have been designed by your firm and form the *Audit Program for Accounts Receivable* on workpapers 21-3 through 21-5. Before continuing, carefully read through the audit program to be sure that you understand the purpose of each audit procedure, including those procedures already completed by Bill Cullen.

Also study the work completed by Bill on workpapers 21-7 through 21-16.

c. Complete step 1 on the audit program (workpaper 21-3).

> **TIP:** The *Planned Tests of Balances Matrix* mentioned in step 1 is found on workpaper 21-6. Bill has completed the first three rows for you.

NOTE: The *Planned Tests of Balances Matrix* summarizes the factors that influence the extent of tests of balances for accounts receivable.

The first factor, acceptable audit risk, is *inversely* related to the extent of testing; i.e., as acceptable audit risk increases, the extent of testing decreases.

Each of the other factors is *directly* related to the extent of testing; e.g., as inherent risk or control risk increases, the extent of testing increases.

Notice that each factor is evaluated separately for each audit objective.

Decide sample size for confirmation of accounts receivable

d.   Use workpaper 21-27, along with the following information, to determine an appropriate sample size for the confirmation of receivables.

There are two unique aspects to determining the sample size using difference estimation. First, the auditor specifies the *acceptable risk of incorrect rejection* (ARIR), as well as the *acceptable risk of incorrect acceptance* (ARIA). Second, the auditor specifies an estimate of the standard deviation of the misstatements expected in the population.

The formula for determining sample size using difference estimation is as follows:

$$n = \left[\frac{SD^* \, (Z_A + Z_R) \, N}{TM - E^*} \right]^2$$

where:

n	=	sample size
SD*	=	estimate of standard deviation of population
Z_A	=	confidence coefficient for ARIA
Z_R	=	confidence coefficient for ARIR
N	=	population size
TM	=	tolerable misstatement for the account
E*	=	estimated population misstatement

Select sample items for testing

e. Independent of your answer in requirement (d), assume your sample size is 35 accounts.

   Use systematic selection to select the sample items for confirmation.

   Use workpaper 21-28 to document your work.

Perform the audit procedures

f. Assume that you mailed 35 confirmations and all have been returned to you from the customers. Five of the 35 customers disagreed with the client regarding the amount owed (see workpapers 21-10 through 21-14). Bill Cullen investigated the differences and wrote explanations on each of these five confirmations. After reading Bill's comments, decide whether the differences are client misstatements and should be projected to the population, or whether they are customer misstatements or timing differences that can be disregarded. Document your decisions by completing the first six columns in the top section of workpaper 21-29.

> **ELECTRONIC WORKPAPER OPTION:** Complete and print workpaper 21-29 using Excel.

Evaluate the results of the tests and conclude whether accounts receivable is fairly stated

g. Workpapers 21-29 through 21-32 are used to summarize the client misstatements found, to project the misstatements to the population, and to decide the acceptability of the account balance.

Complete workpapers 21-29 through 21-32 using the following steps:

> **ELECTRONIC WORKPAPER OPTION:** Complete and print workpapers 21-29 through 21-32 using Excel. Follow these steps:
>
> 1. For each client misstatement in the top section of workpaper 21-29, verify that the formula entered by Bill in column seven correctly calculates the squared misstatement. (For differences not involving a client misstatement, "0" should appear in column seven.) Also verify that columns six and seven have been summed correctly. (When summing column six, overstatements should be treated as positive numbers and understatements as negative numbers.)
>
> 2. Complete the bottom section of workpaper 21-29 to calculate the projected misstatement.
>
> 3. Study the formulas and calculations used by Bill on workpapers 21-30 and 21-31 to determine the sample standard deviation, precision interval, and upper and lower confidence limits. Make corrections if necessary.
>
> Go to step 6 on the next page.

1. Complete column seven in the top section of workpaper 21-29 by calculating the *squared misstatement*. For differences not involving a client misstatement, enter 0 in column seven. Sum the total misstatements (column six) and squared misstatements (column seven). When summing column six, treat overstatements as positive numbers and understatements as negative numbers.

2. Complete the bottom section of workpaper 21-29 to calculate the projected misstatement. Round all amounts to the nearest whole number.

3. Calculate the standard deviation of the sample misstatements in the top section of workpaper 21-30 based on the following formula (round all amounts to the nearest whole number):

$$SD = \sqrt{\frac{\sum (e_j)^2 - n(\bar{e})^2}{n-1}}$$

where:

$\sum e_j$ = summation of individual misstatements in the sample

$\bar{e}$ = mean misstatement in sample

n = sample size

4. Calculate the precision interval in the lower section of workpaper 21-30 using the following formula:

$$CPI = NZ_A \frac{SD}{\sqrt{n}} \sqrt{\frac{N-n}{N}}$$

where:

CPI = computed precision interval

N = population size

Z_A = confidence coefficient for ARIA

The other terms are as described previously.

5. Compute the upper and lower confidence limits in the top section of workpaper 21-31.

6. Complete the bottom half of workpaper 21-31 to document your decision regarding the acceptability of the account balance. You might want to re-read page 5 of this assignment before completing this workpaper.

> **TIP:** Recall that the tolerable misstatement for accounts receivable is $40,000.

7. In the top section of workpaper 21-32, write your conclusion regarding whether accounts receivable is fairly stated or whether further testing will be necessary based on the results of your confirmations of accounts receivable.

h. Complete the bottom section of workpaper 21-32. Refer to the Assignment 6 appendix (Assignment SIX ✦ Page 29) for firm policy regarding the evaluation and disposition of actual and projected misstatements identified during audit testing, including description of the audit misstatement posting threshold. The posting threshold has been set at $2,000 for the Oceanview audit. Misstatements, including projected misstatements, below this amount are considered trivial and do not need to be accumulated. Amounts greater than the audit misstatement threshold should be included on the summary of uncorrected misstatements to determine if the aggregate amount of unadjusted misstatements is material. The projected misstatement should be reduced by the amount of adjusting entries, if any, to accounts receivable by deducting the amount of the adjusting journal entry made to correct the actual misstatements found in your confirmation tests, from the projected misstatement (do not include the adjusting journal entry prepared by Bill Cullen).

Carry forward any unadjusted projected misstatement above the posting threshold to the *Summary of Uncorrected Misstatements* (workpaper 90-1).

> **TIP:** The Identified Misstatement column on workpaper 90-1 includes the amount of any misstatements identified in your testing on workpaper 21-19 that have not been adjusted. Your remaining *unadjusted projected misstatement* on workpaper 21-26 should be entered in the Likely Aggregate Misstatement, Current Assets, and Income Before Taxes columns on workpaper 90-1.

> **NOTE:** Unadjusted actual and projected misstatements are carried forward to the *Summary of Uncorrected Misstatements* (workpaper 90-1).
>
> At the conclusion of the audit, the *Summary of Uncorrected Misstatements* will be reviewed and compared to materiality to decide if further adjusting entries are required to reduce the misstatements to an acceptable level.

i. Assume the client agrees with the adjusting journal entry(ies) proposed on workpaper 21-2.

- Write the net effect (on accounts receivable and the allowance for doubtful accounts) of the entry(ies) in the Net Adjustments column on the accounts receivable leadsheet (workpaper 21-1), and write the new account balance in the 2018 Adjusted Balance column on the leadsheet. You should include the entry already proposed for the allowance for doubtful accounts. Note that Bill has already posted the adjustment to the allowance for doubtful accounts and cross-referenced the balance to workpaper 21-15. You should complete the extensions on the leadsheet, and cross-reference the balance for Account 1100 – accounts receivable. The entry(ies), including the effect on accounts other than accounts receivable, will be posted to the trial balance in Assignment 10.

> **ELECTRONIC WORKPAPER OPTION:** Complete and print workpapers 21-1 and 21-2 using Excel.

j. Complete the conclusion section, step 22, on workpaper 21-5.

Completing the assignment

Make sure you **signed off** on the following workpapers completed in this assignment, using 2/24/2019 as the date: 21-1 through 21-3, 21-5, 21-6, and 21-27 through 21-32.

Also make sure you **signed off** on step 1 on workpaper 21-3 by writing your initials in the INIT column, and added a reference to workpaper 21-6 in the W/P column.

Also make sure you **signed off** on steps 3a, 3b, 3c, and 3d on workpaper 21-3, added references to the appropriate workpapers in the W/P column, and added any necessary explanations in the COMMENTS column.

Group the following items together in the order listed and submit them to your instructor for grading, either in person or online at armonddaltonresources.com (consult your instructor):

- Cover page with your printed name, your signature, and the assignment number.
- Workpapers 21-1 through 21-3, 21-5, 21-6, and 21-27 through 21-32.
- Answers to discussion questions 1 through 6 on the following three pages if required by your instructor.

Discussion questions

1. AICPA auditing standards address the confirmation of accounts receivable for private company audits. What are the circumstances under which confirmation of accounts receivable is *not* required?

_____

_____

_____

_____

_____

_____

_____

2. When confirming accounting receivable, the auditor may use positive confirmations, negative confirmations, or a combination of both. Although the use of negative confirmations is less expensive than positive confirmations, negative confirmations are less reliable. Therefore, negative confirmations should be used only in certain circumstances. Discuss those circumstances.

_____

_____

_____

_____

_____

_____

_____

3. Auditing standards indicate that the auditor should ordinarily presume that there is a risk of material misstatement due to fraud relating to revenue recognition. How might this concern related to revenue recognition affect the nature and extent of confirmation procedures?

_____

_____

_____

_____

_____

_____

4. Responses are often not received for positive accounts receivable confirmation requests. What should the auditor do if a confirmation response is not received?

_____

_____

_____

_____

_____

_____

5. Many differences identified on positive confirmation are timing differences, rather than misstatements. Explain the nature of a timing difference and give examples of common timing differences.

_____

_____

_____

_____

_____

_____

6. Misstatements were identified in the confirmation of accounts receivable. Indicate whether you believe these indicate one or more deficiencies in internal control.

_____

_____

_____

_____

_____

_____

_____

ASSIGNMENT 6: Appendix

LILTS BERGER & ASSOCIATES, CPAs
Ocean City, Florida

POLICY STATEMENT
Title: Evaluation and Disposition of Misstatements

Professional judgment is to be used at all times in evaluating misstatements found in audit testing. In addition to the dollar amount of the misstatement, factors to consider include whether the amount is a known or likely misstatement based on a sample, or a likely misstatement of a client estimate. The nature of the misstatement must also be considered, including whether the misstatement is due to error or fraud. It is also necessary to evaluate whether the misstatement is indicative of a deficiency in internal control, and whether additional testing is necessary to accumulate sufficient appropriate audit evidence.

As a general guideline, the following policies are to be applied:

1. Misstatements greater than performance materiality — An audit adjustment should normally be proposed for misstatements greater than performance materiality.

2. Misstatements greater than the audit misstatement posting threshold and less than performance materiality — Misstatements less than performance materiality and greater than the audit misstatement posting threshold should normally be accumulated on the summary of uncorrected misstatements to assess whether the aggregate amount of uncorrected misstatements is material to the financial statements. Clients should be encouraged to record an adjustment for known misstatements, especially amounts that are greater than 50% of performance materiality.

3. Amounts less than the audit misstatement posting threshold — Amounts less than the audit misstatement posting threshold are usually ignored as clearly trivial, unless other factors are present that suggest the need for further consideration.

Audit Misstatement Posting Threshold

The audit misstatement posting threshold is an amount set by the auditor to determine whether a misstatement is clearly trivial and can be ignored as immaterial. Amounts greater than the posting threshold but less than performance materiality should be accumulated on the summary of uncorrected misstatements to determine if the combined aggregate amount of misstatements is material (amounts greater than performance materiality normally require a proposed audit adjustment). The posting threshold should normally be set at 3% of the preliminary judgment of materiality. Actual and projected misstatements below this amount can be passed as immaterial, and misstatements above this amount should be accumulated on the summary of uncorrected misstatements.

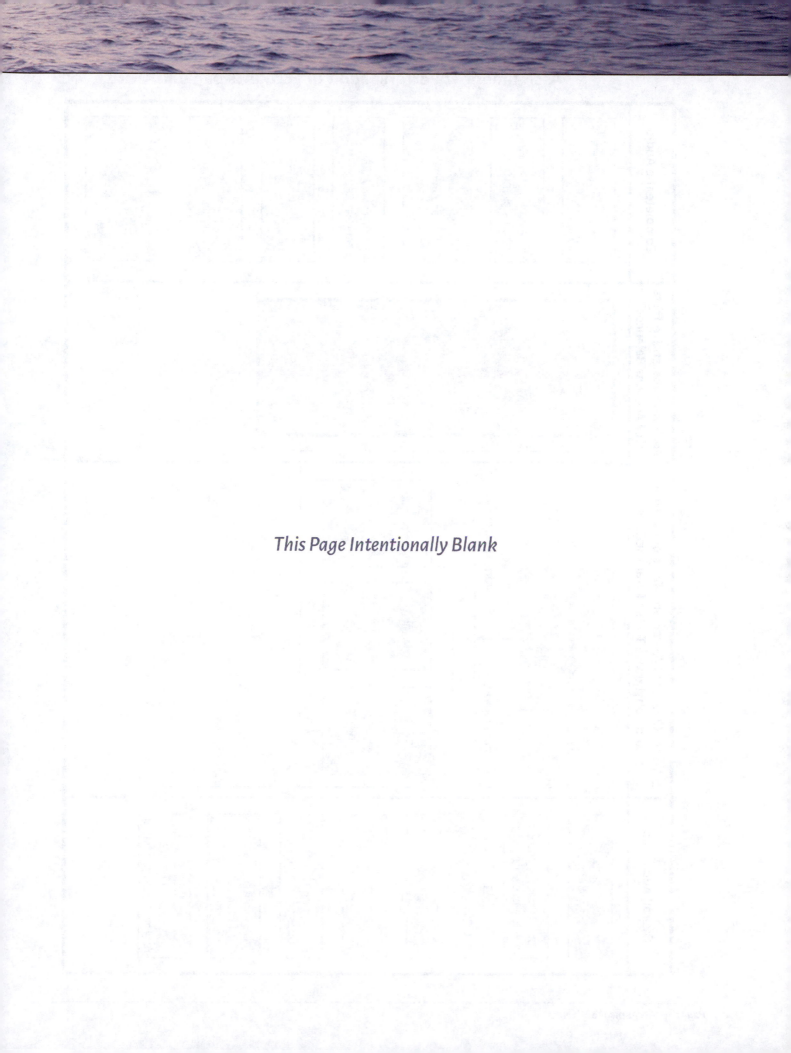

This Page Intentionally Blank

Assignment 7: Perform audit of accounts payable

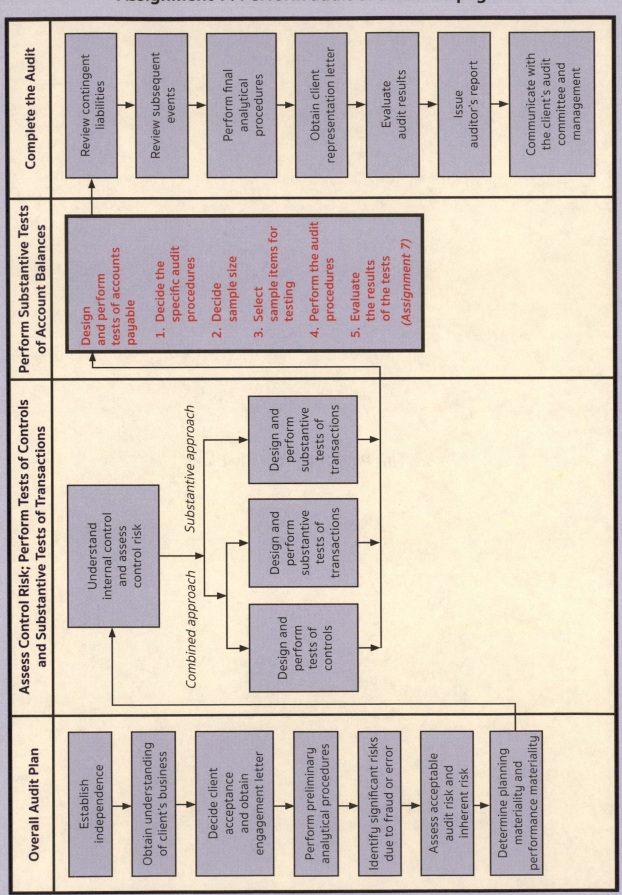

Complete the Audit

- Review contingent liabilities
- Review subsequent events
- Perform final analytical procedures
- Obtain client representation letter
- Evaluate audit results
- Issue auditor's report
- Communicate with the client's audit committee and management

Perform Substantive Tests of Account Balances

Design and perform tests of accounts payable

1. Decide the specific audit procedures
2. Decide sample size
3. Select sample items for testing
4. Perform the audit procedures
5. Evaluate the results of the tests *(Assignment 7)*

Assess Control Risk; Perform Tests of Controls and Substantive Tests of Transactions

Understand internal control and assess control risk

Substantive approach

Design and perform substantive tests of transactions

Combined approach

Design and perform substantive tests of transactions

Design and perform tests of controls

Overall Audit Plan

- Establish independence
- Obtain understanding of client's business
- Decide client acceptance and obtain engagement letter
- Perform preliminary analytical procedures
- Identify significant risks due to fraud or error
- Assess acceptable audit risk and inherent risk
- Determine planning materiality and performance materiality

ASSIGNMENT 7: Perform audit of accounts payable

Overview

In this assignment, you will audit Oceanview Marine Company's accounts payable balance.

There are five closely related steps in the audit of accounts payable:

1. Decide the specific audit procedures to be performed for each audit objective.
2. Decide the sample size for each audit procedure.
3. Select sample items for testing.
4. Perform the audit procedures for the sample items.
5. Evaluate the results of the tests and conclude whether the accounts payable balance is fairly stated.

Auditing concepts

Nature of the audit of accounts payable

The audit of the year-end accounts payable balance involves accumulating sufficient appropriate evidence to evaluate whether accounts payable is fairly stated and properly disclosed in the financial statements. Although the auditor is concerned with whether recorded accounts payable exist and are accurately recorded, the primary concerns are whether the accounts payable balance is complete and whether an accurate cutoff of accounts payable has been achieved.

The primary audit procedure performed to determine the completeness of the accounts payable balance is the search for unrecorded liabilities. This involves examining cash disbursements after year-end and unpaid invoices to determine whether they represent liabilities as of the balance sheet date. The search for unrecorded liabilities may also include tracing receiving reports issued before year-end to vendor invoices, tracing vendor statements to the accounts payable trial balance, and sending confirmations to vendors with which the client does business. Because of the availability of external documentation such as vendor invoices and statements, confirmation of accounts payable is less common than confirmation of accounts receivable.

Performing the search for unrecorded liabilities

In Assignment 6, you used sampling to perform tests of the recorded accounts receivable balance. Because the focus of the search for unrecorded liabilities is on omitted payables, it is difficult to define the population and determine the population size in accounts payable. For this reason, auditors generally select specific items for testing when performing the search for unrecorded liabilities.

Auditors follow these steps to perform tests of accounts payable:

1. **Plan the test**

   Audit procedures are designed for each audit objective (i.e., existence, completeness, accuracy, cutoff, and so on). The most important audit procedure for accounts payable is the search for unrecorded liabilities, which helps satisfy the *completeness* and *cutoff* objectives. As part of performing these procedures, the auditor also obtains evidence related to the existence and accuracy of accounts payable.

2. **Determine the items to be tested**

   Although the search for unrecorded liabilities usually involves testing of specific items rather than audit sampling, several factors are considered when determining the number of items to tests. These factors include:

   - *Performance materiality*—performance materiality has a significant impact on the amount of testing performed. Auditors generally test all items greater than performance materiality, and may test a judgmental selection of items below performance materiality.
   - *Expected misstatement in the population*—if misstatements are expected, the auditor may decide to use an amount lower than performance materiality to identify items to be tested, and may select a greater number of smaller items for testing.
   - *Control risk* (after performing tests of controls)—higher control risk increases required assurance and the extent of substantive testing of the accounts payable balance.
   - *Inherent risk*—higher inherent risk increases required assurance and the extent of testing.
   - *Acceptable audit risk*—lower acceptable audit risk increases required assurance and the extent of testing.
   - *Results of preliminary analytical procedures*—if the results of preliminary analytical procedures indicate a high potential for misstatements in accounts payable, required assurance and the extent of testing would increase.
   - *Results of substantive tests of transactions*—if the results of substantive tests of transactions for acquisitions and cash disbursements indicate a high potential for misstatements in accounts payable, required assurance and the extent of testing would increase.

   There are alternative ways for auditors to assess these factors. The items to be tested in this assignment will be determined judgmentally, giving adequate consideration to the factors described above. All items greater than performance materiality will be selected for testing, plus a judgmental number of items less than or equal to performance materiality.

3. **Select items for testing**

   In the search for unrecorded liabilities, the emphasis is on large amounts recorded in the acquisitions and cash disbursements journals during the first month after year-end. Auditors often select all items greater than performance materiality, and a judgmental number of items below performance materiality.

4. **Perform the audit procedures**

The most time-consuming part of auditing accounts payable or any other account is performing the tests. When auditing accounts payable, these tests include examining receiving reports, other supporting documents, and journal entries to determine whether all liabilities have been recorded, whether they have been recorded in the proper period, and whether they have been recorded at the correct amounts. Goods or services received before year-end should generally be included in accounts payable at year-end, while those received after year-end should be excluded from accounts payable.

5. **Evaluate the results of the tests and conclude whether the accounts payable balance is fairly stated**

When the auditor evaluates the results of the tests for an account such as accounts payable, the primary objective is to decide whether the account is fairly stated or is materially misstated. The auditor must also decide whether prior assessments of control risk and inherent risk require revision based on the results of the tests of balances.

There are several possible actions after the auditor evaluates the results of the search for unrecorded liabilities:

- *Accept the population as stated.* This conclusion is likely if the misstatements found are less than performance materiality, giving adequate consideration to the number and dollar amount of items tested.
- *Request the client to adjust the population.* Auditors should always inform their clients of any misstatements found in an account balance. If the account is not acceptable as stated, an adjusting journal entry to correct the misstatements may make the account acceptable.
- *Expand audit tests.* If neither of the first two options applies, the auditor may expand substantive tests of balances, either by increasing the number of items tested or performing other tests.
- *Request that the client re-work the population.* In rare cases, the client might need to determine the account balance again. If this is necessary, the auditor will need to re-audit the population.

Analyze misstatements and reassess risks. Regardless of whether the auditor accepts or rejects the recorded account balance, the auditor should determine the nature and cause of every misstatement found in the sample. Normally, if performance materiality is significantly greater than the identified misstatements, it is unnecessary to expand the audit tests beyond those originally planned. The auditor may decide that the original assessment of control risk or inherent risk may require revision, given the findings of the substantive tests.

Requirements

a. In preparation for this assignment, obtain the following from the *Current Workpapers*: 30-1, 30-2, 30-4, 30-5, 30-21, 30-22, and 30-23.

These workpapers will be completed in this assignment and turned in to your instructor for grading. Remember to **sign off** on each workpaper as you complete it. Use 2/25/2019 as the completion date for each workpaper you complete in this assignment.

> **ELECTRONIC WORKPAPER OPTION:** In this assignment, you can complete and print workpapers 30-1, 30-2, and 30-21 through 30-23 using Excel. **These workpapers are included in the file named "Assign 7 Excel_7ed.xlsx."** You may disregard the copies of these workpapers included in the *Current Workpapers*.

Plan the tests

b. Specific audit procedures for accounts payable have been designed by your firm and form the audit program on workpapers 30-3 through 30-5. Before continuing, carefully read through the audit program to be sure that you understand the purpose of each audit procedure, including those procedures already completed by Bill Cullen.

c. Review the Planned Tests of Balances Matrix for accounts payable (workpaper 30-6) completed by Bill.

> **NOTE:** The matrix summarizes the factors that influence the extent of tests of balances for accounts payable.
>
> The first factor, acceptable audit risk, is *inversely* related to the extent of testing; i.e., as acceptable audit risk increases, the extent of testing decreases.
>
> Each of the other factors is *directly* related to the extent of testing; e.g., as inherent risk or control risk increases, the extent of testing increases.
>
> Notice that each factor is evaluated separately for each audit objective.

Also study the work completed by Bill on workpapers 30-7 to 30-19.

Decide items to be tested in search for unrecorded liabilities

d. Your primary responsibility in this assignment is to complete steps 4(b) through 4(e) on workpaper 30-4. Bill has already determined the extent of testing for the tests of subsequent cash disbursements [step 4(a)].

Study workpaper 30-20 to learn how Bill determined the number of items to be tested.

> **NOTE:** Notice that Bill used his judgment in determining the number of items to test, incorporating information about performance materiality, expected misstatements, acceptable audit risk, inherent risk, control risk, and results of analytical procedures.

> **NOTE:** The search for unrecorded liabilities involves testing of subsequent cash disbursements, as well as testing purchases recorded in the acquisitions journal after year-end, and invoices which have not yet been recorded in the acquisitions journal. The purpose of examining each type of transaction is to determine whether any liabilities have been omitted from the year-end list of accounts payable. Because the objective of each test is the same, testing is limited to January cash disbursements in this practice case. Because many disbursements after year-end will represent payments against valid accounts payable included in the year-end accounts payable listing, the accuracy of amounts in the year-end list of accounts payable can be tested simultaneously with the test for omitted liabilities.

Select items for testing

e. As determined in step (d), the items to be tested consist of the following:

   - All 20 disbursements greater than performance materiality.
   - A judgmental selection of 15 of the remaining 134 disbursements.

> **ELECTRONIC WORKPAPER OPTION:** Complete and print workpaper 30-21 using Excel.

Indicate the second, third, and fourth cash disbursements selected for testing in each group of items on workpaper 30-21.

> **TIPS:** Select the disbursements to be tested from the list of cash disbursements (check register) beginning on workpaper 30-11.
>
> For the first set of items, you should select only disbursements that exceed performance materiality.
>
> For the amounts to be tested less than or equal to performance materiality, select every eighth disbursement beginning with the third disbursement. In making these selections, be sure to exclude the disbursements greater than performance materiality that have already been selected.
>
> Since the items to be tested are being drawn from subsequent cash disbursements, the selections should be drawn from the disbursements (check totals), rather than the individual voucher amounts that make up each disbursement.

Perform the audit procedures

f. Assume that Bill has examined the supporting documents for 29 of the 35 subsequent cash disbursements selected for testing and found no misstatements.

To complete the tests for omitted liabilities, you are to examine the supporting documents for the remaining six cash disbursements and trace each disbursement representing a liability at year-end to the year-end Accounts Payable List (workpapers 30-7 through 30-10).

Write appropriate tickmarks on the year-end Accounts Payable List (workpapers 30-7 through 30-10) and on the Check Register (workpapers 30-11 through 30-18) to indicate the work you performed and the results. (Use the tickmarks created by Bill; see tickmarks "d" and "e" on workpaper 30-19 and tickmark "d" on workpaper 30-10. You will need to create additional tickmarks if you discover any misstatements.)

Document any misstatements you find by completing the Summary of Misstatements sections on workpaper 30-22.

> **ELECTRONIC WORKPAPER OPTION:** Use Excel workpapers 30-22 and 30-23 to complete steps (f) and (g).

TIPS: The six disbursements you will test are the same as the second, third, and fourth cash disbursements selected in each part of the sample on workpaper 30-21.

You are testing the six cash disbursements to determine (1) that those disbursements that represent accounts payable at December 31 were properly included in the year-end list of accounts payable and (2) that those disbursements that did *not* represent liabilities at December 31 were properly excluded from the year-end list of accounts payable.

You will use the following documents as you trace each of the six disbursements to the year-end accounts payable list: receiving reports for Tradewind Marine, Great Outdoor Boats, Lift King, and Anderson Marine (two), and the invoice for Salt, Sand & Sea Advertising. All receiving reports are for inventory, except the receiving report from Lift King, which is for a fixed asset. For Anderson Marine, receiving report #5895 relates to check #6281, and receiving report #5901 relates to check #6298. These documents are included in the *Client Documents* folder.

For each payment for a purchase of goods, you need to examine the date on the related receiving report to determine whether the purchase created a liability as of December 31. Assume all shipments from vendors are shipped FOB destination (title passes, and the liability is created, when the goods are received by Oceanview). For each payment for a service, you need to examine the related invoice to determine the date the service was received by Oceanview.

When calculating the net misstatement on workpaper 30-22, overstatements should be treated as positive numbers and understatements as negative numbers.

Evaluate the results of the tests and conclude whether accounts payable is fairly stated

g. Workpaper 30-22 is used to summarize the client misstatements detected, and workpaper 30-23 is used to decide the acceptability of the account balance using your professional judgment.

> **NOTE:** To ensure adequate coverage of accounts payable testing, Bill selected all items greater than performance materiality, and a judgmental number of the remaining disbursements (see workpaper 30-20).

Complete workpaper 30-23 using the following steps:

1. Carry forward the total misstatements from workpaper 30-22 to the bottom of workpaper 30-23.

2. Using your professional judgment, decide whether to:

    - accept the population as fairly stated,
    - request the client adjust the account,
    - expand your audit tests of accounts payable, or
    - request the client re-work the account.

    Re-read step 5 of the testing steps earlier in this assignment for clarification of this process.

    Use workpaper 30-23 to document and justify your decision.

3. In the middle section of workpaper 30-23, write your conclusions regarding whether accounts payable is fairly stated or whether further testing will be necessary based on the results of your tests.

h. Use workpaper 30-2 to propose any adjusting journal entry(ies) to correct the actual misstatement(s) found in your tests.

> **TIP:** You may wish to refer to the firm's policy statement in the appendix to Assignment 6 (Assignment SIX ✦ Page 29) to determine the appropriate treatment of the misstatements. An adjustment should normally be proposed for misstatements greater than performance materiality. Amounts below performance materiality but above the misstatement posting threshold should be accumulated on workpaper 90-1, Summary of Uncorrected Misstatements. Amounts below the posting threshold (set at $2,000 for the Oceanview Marine audit) can normally be regarded as trivial and do not need to be accumulated.

i. Assume the client has agreed to record your proposed adjusting journal entry(ies). Write the net effect of your entry(ies) in the Net Adjustments column on the accounts payable leadsheet (workpaper 30-1) and on the leadsheet(s) (if included as part of this practice case) of the other account(s) affected by your adjusting journal entry(ies). Write the new account balance in the 2018 Adjusted Balance column on the leadsheet(s). The entry(ies) will be posted to the trial balance in Assignment 10.

Cross-reference the Adjusting Journal Entries workpaper (30-2) to the adjustment(s) shown on the accounts payable leadsheet (30-1) and the other leadsheets affected.

j. Complete the bottom section of workpaper 30-23 by deducting from the total misstatement the net effect on accounts payable of any adjusting journal entry on workpaper 30-2.

Carry forward any remaining unadjusted misstatement to the *Summary of Uncorrected Misstatements* (workpaper 90-1) if greater than the posting threshold of $2,000.

At the end of the audit, workpaper 90-1 will be reviewed and compared to materiality to determine if further adjusting entries are required to reduce the misstatements to an acceptable level.

> **NOTE: Unadjusted** misstatements are carried forward to the *Summary of Uncorrected Misstatements* (workpaper 90-1). If your adjusting journal entries had not been recorded at this time, then the actual misstatements you discovered in your tests of accounts payable would have been carried forward to the *Summary of Uncorrected Misstatements*.

k. Complete the conclusion section, step 9, on workpaper 30-5.

Completing the assignment

Make sure you **signed off** on the following workpapers completed in this assignment, using 2/25/2019 as the date: 30-1, 30-2, 30-4, 30-5, 30-21, 30-22, and 30-23.

Also make sure you **signed off** on step 4, sub-steps (b) through (e), on workpaper 30-4 by writing your initials in the INIT column, added a reference to workpapers 30-21 to 30-23 in the W/P column, and added *"Items selected per 30-21"* in the COMMENTS column next to step (b).

Group the following items together in the order listed and submit them to your instructor for grading, either in person or online at armonddaltonresources.com:

- Cover page with your printed name, your signature, and the assignment number.
- Workpapers 30-1, 30-2, 30-4, 30-5, 30-7 through 30-10, 30-21, 30-22, and 30-23.
- Answers to discussion questions 1 through 5 (see next three pages) if required by your instructor.

Discussion questions

1. In Assignment 5, you performed tests of controls and substantive tests of transactions for acquisitions. How do the results of those tests affect the extent of testing in the audit of accounts payable?

_____

_____

_____

_____

_____

_____

2. What are the primary objectives in the audit of accounts payable? How did this affect the testing method used, and how the results were evaluated compared to your tests of accounts receivable?

_____

_____

_____

_____

_____

_____

_____

3. The client received and recorded a large shipment of inventory on January 3 that was shipped FOB shipping point on December 29. How should the auditor account for this in the search for unrecorded liabilities?

_____

_____

_____

_____

_____

_____

4. Confirmations were emphasized in tests of accounts receivable, but are rarely used in tests of accounts payable. What factors account for this difference? When would confirmation of accounts payable be appropriate?

_____

_____

_____

_____

_____

_____

_____

_____

5. The client received a shipment of inventory late on December 31 after the physical inventory count was completed. Because the inventory was not recorded at year-end, the client also did not record the related liability until January. How might the auditor detect this misstatement? Assume the purchase was for inventory with a cost of $40,000. What is the effect on accounts payable and net income in the year under audit due to the failure to record this transaction?

    _____

    _____

    _____

    _____

    _____

    _____

    _____

Assignment 8: Perform audit of cash

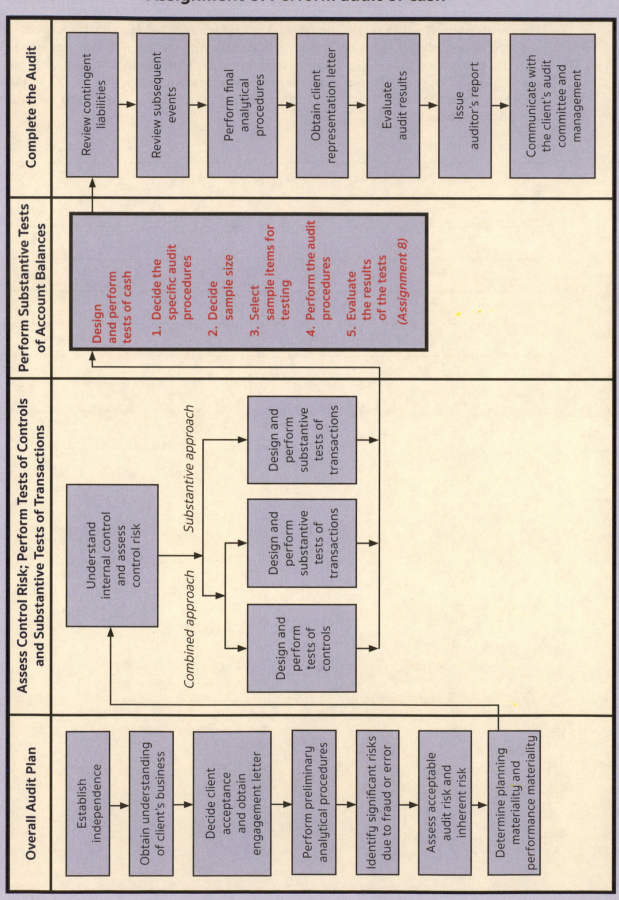

Overall Audit Plan

- Establish independence
- Obtain understanding of client's business
- Decide client acceptance and obtain engagement letter
- Perform preliminary analytical procedures
- Identify significant risks due to fraud or error
- Assess acceptable audit risk and inherent risk
- Determine planning materiality and performance materiality

Assess Control Risk; Perform Tests of Controls and Substantive Tests of Transactions

- Understand internal control and assess control risk
- *Substantive approach*
  - Design and perform substantive tests of transactions
- *Combined approach*
  - Design and perform substantive tests of transactions
  - Design and perform tests of controls

Perform Substantive Tests of Account Balances

Design and perform tests of cash
1. Decide the specific audit procedures
2. Decide sample size
3. Select sample items for testing
4. Perform the audit procedures
5. Evaluate the results of the tests
(Assignment 8)

Complete the Audit

- Review contingent liabilities
- Review subsequent events
- Perform final analytical procedures
- Obtain client representation letter
- Evaluate audit results
- Issue auditor's report
- Communicate with the client's audit committee and management

ASSIGNMENT 8: Perform audit of cash

Overview

⚓ In this assignment you will audit Oceanview Marine Company's general bank account.

Auditing concepts

Audit of cash balances

The audit of year-end cash balances involves accumulating sufficient appropriate evidence to evaluate whether cash balances are fairly stated and properly disclosed in the financial statements. To determine the extent of testing of cash, the auditor must evaluate internal controls over cash. Examples of these controls include but are not limited to:

- proper segregation of duties
- the signing of checks or approval of electronic payments by an authorized person
- the use of prenumbered checks
- the use of a prelisting of cash receipts
- a monthly reconciliation of all bank accounts by someone independent of the handling or recording of cash receipts and cash disbursements.

If the auditor determines that the internal controls over cash are inadequate, he or she will most likely extend the year-end audit procedures to include one or more of the following items: extended tests of bank reconciliations, a proof of cash, and other procedures that may detect possible fraud. The audit procedures discussed in the following sections apply when the auditor has identified no significant deficiencies in the internal controls over cash.

General and imprest payroll cash accounts

To begin the audit of cash accounts, the auditor obtains from the client a year-end bank reconciliation for each bank account. Most audit procedures are limited to obtaining assurance that the information on the bank reconciliation is correct. Typical audit procedures include:

- Test the clerical accuracy of the client's bank reconciliation, including outstanding checks, deposits in transit, and other reconciling items.
- Confirm the cash balance directly with the client's bank and reconcile the balance given by the bank with the bank balance shown on the bank reconciliation. The confirmation may be sent by mail or electronically through a third-party intermediary.
- Agree the book balance from the bank reconciliation to the general ledger.
- Request that a cutoff bank statement, along with copies of canceled checks, be sent directly from the bank to the auditor for a 7- to 10-day period after the client's balance sheet date. Some auditors use online electronic access to the client's bank account activity in place of a cutoff bank statement.

- Trace checks received with the cutoff bank statement dated on or before the balance sheet date to the list of outstanding checks on the bank reconciliation.
- Investigate any significant checks listed on the bank reconciliation that did not clear the bank as of the cutoff statement date.
- Agree deposits in transit on the bank reconciliation to the cutoff bank statement and verify other reconciling items.
- Test the client's schedule of intercompany and interbank transfers for a few days before and after the balance sheet date and determine that each transfer was recorded in the proper period for both accounts.

When analyzing a schedule of intercompany and interbank transfers, you should also verify that each partially completed transfer at year-end is properly reflected in the bank reconciliation(s).

For example, assume the balance sheet date is 12/31/2018. If, for one of the transfers shown on the schedule of interbank transfers, the date per books and the date per bank for the disbursing account were 12/27/2018 and 1/5/2019, respectively, then the transfer is an outstanding item (check or wire transfer) at year-end. You would trace the transfer to the year-end bank reconciliation for the disbursing account to verify that the transfer appears in the list of outstanding items. The transfer should then be cross-referenced from the schedule of transfers to the outstanding item on the bank reconciliation.

Similarly, if the dates per books and bank for the receiving account were 12/27/2018 and 1/5/2019, respectively, then the transfer is a deposit-in-transit at year-end. You would agree and cross-reference the transfer to the year-end bank reconciliation for the receiving account to verify that the deposit-in-transit appears on the reconciliation.

If the dates per books and bank for the disbursing account were 1/5/2019 and 12/27/2018, respectively, then the transfer is an unrecorded disbursement at year-end. You would agree and cross-reference the transfer to the year-end bank reconciliation for the disbursing account to verify that the reconciliation contains an adjustment to the balance per books to reflect the unrecorded disbursement.

Similarly, if the dates per books and bank for the receiving account were 1/5/2019 and 12/27/2018, respectively, then the transfer is an unrecorded deposit at year-end. You would agree and cross-reference the transfer to the year-end bank reconciliation for the receiving account to verify that the reconciliation contains an adjustment to the balance per books to reflect the unrecorded deposit.

Background information

Oceanview's cash balance includes the following accounts: petty cash, payroll bank account, and general bank account. Bill Cullen performed all of the audit program procedures for cash except steps 9, 10, 11, 12, 13, and 16 on workpapers 20-2 and 20-3. He completed these steps for the payroll bank account but did not perform them for the general bank account. Bill also did not complete step 19 on workpaper 20-4.

Requirements

a. In preparation for this assignment, obtain the following from the *Current Workpapers:* 20-1, 20-2, 20-3, 20-4, 20-6, 20-7, and 20-8.

These workpapers will be completed in this assignment and submitted to your instructor for grading. Remember to **sign off** on each workpaper as you complete it. Use 2/25/2019 as the completion date for each workpaper you complete in this assignment.

> **ELECTRONIC WORKPAPER OPTION:** In this assignment, you can complete and print workpapers 20-1, 20-5, and 20-6 using Microsoft Excel. **These workpapers are included in the file named "Assign 8 Excel_7ed.xlsx."** You may disregard the copies of these workpapers in the *Current Workpapers*.
>
> To prevent accidental modifications of the Excel file, each sheet has been "protected." If you need to make changes to a sheet, you will need to first unprotect the sheet by clicking on REVIEW, UNPROTECT SHEET.

> **NOTE:** On workpaper 20-1, notice that Bill has agreed the figures for petty cash, the payroll bank account, and the general bank account to the general ledger, and has also agreed all three amounts for 2017 to the prior year's workpapers file. Bill also cross-referenced the balance per books on workpaper 20-5 to workpaper 20-1.

b. Bill Cullen has completed the audit of Oceanview's payroll bank account.

Study workpapers 20-2 to 20-5 to familiarize yourself with the work already performed by Bill.

> **NOTE:** The cutoff bank statements for the payroll account and the general bank account are located at the back of the *Client Documents* folder. (Assume that Bill Cullen received the cutoff bank statements directly from the bank, and that they will be given to the client when the auditors are finished with them. Accordingly, when using the cutoff statements in the following steps, you should not write any tickmarks on them.)

c. Make sure the unadjusted balance per books on workpaper 20-6 agrees with the 2018 balance shown on workpaper 20-1.

Complete steps 9, 10, 11, 12, and 13 on workpapers 20-2 and 20-3 for the general cash account.

> **TIP:** Use workpapers 20-6 and 20-7 to document your work. Use workpaper 20-5 as a guide. Create additional tickmarks as needed.
>
> As you perform step 9, write the tickmark "F" below each column of numbers on the reconciliation (workpaper 20-6) after you verify the numbers have been added (or subtracted) correctly.
>
> When performing step 11, keep in mind that the last check written in 2018 was #6269.
>
> When performing step 12, assume that you reviewed the January 2019 monthly bank statement to investigate checks that had not cleared the bank by the cutoff statement date (January 8, 2019). Also assume that all such checks cleared by January 31, 2019, and appeared on the January 2019 bank statement.

   d.   Complete steps 16a, 16b, and 16d on workpaper 20-3.

> **TIP:** Bill has already verified that the dates, amounts, and payee and payor information on the transfer schedule are correct.
>
> You should analyze the pattern of dates for each transfer to determine whether kiting has occurred (see workpaper 20-8).
>
> In addition, you should determine whether each transfer has been handled properly on the bank reconciliation for each account. For guidance, review the notes on "General and imprest payroll cash accounts" in the Auditing Concepts section earlier in this assignment.
>
> Document your performance of step 16a by writing your initials in the INIT column on workpaper 20-3. Briefly summarize the results of your procedure in the COMMENTS column.
>
> As you perform step 16b, write the appropriate workpaper reference(s) below the amount(s) on the transfer schedule (workpaper 20-8).
>
> As you perform step 16d, document your procedure by creating a new tickmark. In the tickmark legend on the bottom of workpaper 20-8, write an explanation for the tickmark you create.

   e.   Complete the conclusion, step 19, on workpaper 20-4.

   f.   Write the net effect of any adjustments you believe should be made to the year-end cash balances in the Net Adjustments column on the cash leadsheet (workpaper 20-1), and complete the 2018 Adjusted Balance column. (If no adjustments are needed, enter "0" in the Net Adjustments column.)

Completing the assignment

Make sure you **signed off** on the following workpapers completed in this assignment, using 2/25/2019 as the date: 20-1 through 20-4 and 20-6 through 20-8.

Also make sure you **signed off** on workpapers 20-2 and 20-3, steps 9, 10, 11, 12, 13, and 16 by writing your initials in the INIT column, added references to appropriate workpapers in the W/P column, and added any appropriate comments in the COMMENTS column.

Group the following items together in the order listed and submit them to your instructor for grading, either in person or online at armonddaltonresources.com (consult your instructor):

- Cover page with your printed name, your signature, and the assignment number.
- Workpapers 20-1, 20-2, 20-3, 20-4, 20-6, 20-7, and 20-8.
- Answers to discussion questions 1 through 6 (see next four pages) if required by your instructor.

Discussion questions

1. Auditors send bank confirmations for most active bank accounts. Are bank confirmations required under AICPA or PCAOB auditing standards? How does this compare to the requirements for confirmation of accounts receivable?

_____

_____

_____

_____

_____

_____

_____

_____

_____

_____

2. What is the primary purpose of a bank confirmation? Why does the auditor confirm the bank balance in addition to agreeing the year-end bank balance to the bank statement? What additional information is included with a standard bank confirmation?

_____

_____

_____

_____

_____

_____

_____

_____

_____

_____

3. Bank confirmations are often sent electronically using a third-party intermediary. The auditor transmits the request to the intermediary, which then transmits the request to the bank. What are the advantages of using a third-party to send confirmations electronically?

_____

_____

_____

_____

_____

_____

_____

_____

_____

4. Suppose there were several large outstanding checks on the year-end bank reconciliation that did not clear the bank by the cutoff date. Discuss the possible cause(s) of this, and discuss the nature of the potential misstatement(s) that could result.

_____

_____

_____

_____

_____

_____

_____

_____

_____

_____

_____

5. Suppose there was a deposit-in-transit on the year-end bank reconciliation that was not received by the bank by the cutoff date. Discuss the possible cause(s) of this, and discuss the nature of the potential misstatement(s) that could result.

_____

_____

_____

_____

_____

_____

_____

_____

_____

_____

_____

6. Refer to workpaper 20-8. Suppose there was a third transfer on the interbank transfer schedule for $16,500. Assume that the funds were transferred from the general cash account to the payroll cash account. Also assume that the transfer was recorded in the client's cash disbursements journal on 1/4/2019, and the check cleared the disbursing bank on 1/4/2019. In addition, assume that the transfer was recorded in the client's cash receipts journal on 12/26/2018 and was received by the receiving bank on 12/26/2018. Discuss the concerns you would have about this transfer.

_____

_____

_____

_____

_____

_____

_____

Assignment 9: Perform audit of inventory

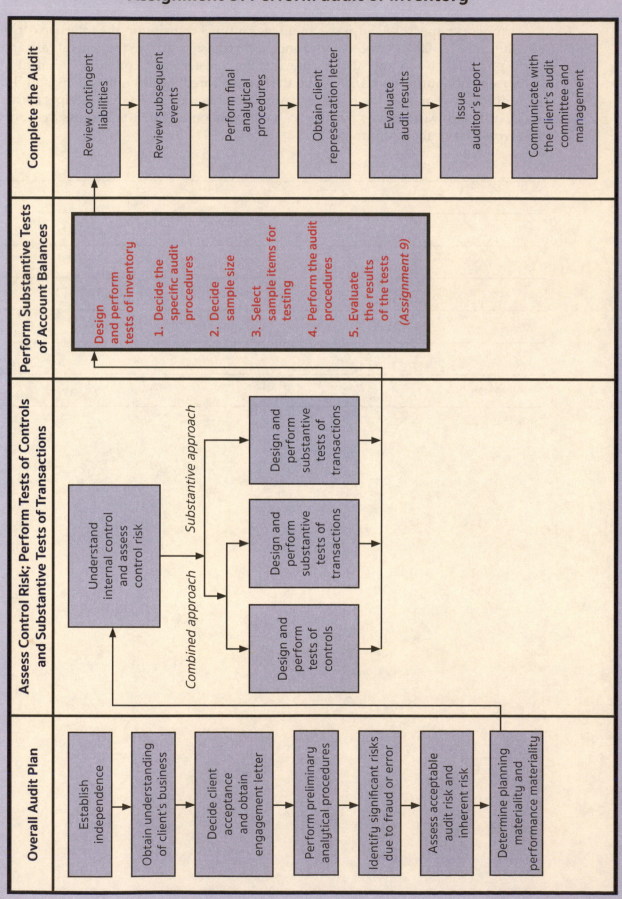

ASSIGNMENT 9 : Perform audit of inventory

Overview

⚓ In this assignment you will audit Oceanview Marine Company's inventory account.

Auditing concepts

Nature of the audit of inventory

The audit of the year-end inventory balances involves accumulating sufficient appropriate evidence to evaluate whether inventory balances are fairly stated and properly disclosed in the financial statements. To plan the appropriate extent of testing, the auditor must evaluate internal controls over inventory. Examples of these controls include but are not limited to:

- authorization of purchase orders by an appropriate person
- the maintenance of inventory records by someone independent of the custody of inventory
- periodic inventory counts
- documents authorizing the movement of inventory

If the auditor determines that internal controls over inventory are inadequate, he or she will most likely extend the year-end audit procedures to include more emphasis on the observation of the inventory count, including cutoff procedures and the valuation of the inventory.

Checking cutoff accuracy involves examining receiving reports prior to and after the count date to ensure all major items are correctly included in the inventory count if received prior to the count or excluded, if after. The receiving reports should also be checked to purchases and payables accounting records for an accurate cutoff in the general ledger. The last few shipping documents prepared prior to the count should be checked to ensure these goods are excluded from inventory, and that goods shipped after year-end are included in year-end inventory.

Even if the internal controls over inventory appear to be adequate, it is often more cost efficient not to perform tests of controls but to rely on extended substantive procedures and the year-end inventory count. This assignment assumes that relying on extended substantive procedures is the approach that will be taken for the audit of inventory.

Background information

Oceanview's inventory includes new boats, used boats, repair parts, and marine supplies. Bill Cullen performed all of the inventory audit program procedures except steps 32, 33, and 38 on workpapers 22-6 and 22-7.

Bill Cullen tested the repair parts and marine supplies inventory. Due to the bulkiness of the final listings, they have been filed in a separate file. No misstatements were found. You are to audit only the boat inventory listed on workpapers 22-8 through 22-10.

Requirements

a. In preparation for this assignment, obtain the following from the *Current Workpapers*: 22-1, 22-6, 22-7, 22-15, 22-18, and 22-19.

These workpapers will be completed in this assignment and turned in to your instructor for grading. Remember to **sign off** on each workpaper as you complete it. Use 2/25/2019 as the completion date for each workpaper you complete in this assignment.

> **ELECTRONIC WORKPAPER OPTION:** In this assignment, you can complete and print workpapers 22-1 and 22-18 using Microsoft Excel. **These workpapers are included in the file named "Assign 9 Excel_7ed.xlsx."** You may disregard the copies of these workpapers in the *Current Workpapers*.

> **NOTE:** On workpaper 22-1, notice that Bill has agreed the figures for each inventory category to the general ledger. The testing of repair parts and supplies is complete, and the adjusted balance has been cross-referenced to workpaper 22-10. Bill has also agreed the amounts for 2017 to the prior year's workpaper file.

b. Study workpapers 22-3 through 22-7 to gain a better understanding of the audit procedures required to audit the inventory account.

> **NOTE:** Bill Cullen observed the physical inventory count performed at year-end, completed the *physical inventory count* section of the audit program (workpapers 22-3 and 22-4) and found no discrepancies except for the provision for obsolete items.
>
> As shown on workpaper 22-11, Bill noted $10,900.00 of repair parts and supplies that were obsolete. Although these items were all very old, Don Phillips did not believe that an adjustment was required as he felt that "these things will come in handy someday."
>
> Since Bill and Don could not agree on this issue, Bill decided to carry this amount forward to the *Summary of Uncorrected Misstatements* (workpaper 90-1).

c. Perform audit program procedure 32 on workpaper 22-6 by following steps one and two described on the next page.

> **TIP:** You are to gain assurance that all the boats counted by the client as listed on their Inventory Count Sheet (workpapers 22-12 through 22-14) appear on the Final Inventory Listing (workpapers 22-8 through 22-10) (testing the completeness assertion), and that all boats that appear on the final inventory listing are in the possession of the client (testing the existence assertion).
>
> This is done by selecting a sample of boats *from* the count sheet and comparing *to* the final inventory listing, and vice versa, as described on the next page.

> **NOTE:** The two-way test count tracing described earlier is often performed when a detailed inventory listing is not available at the time of the physical observation. Assume that a listing was not available at the time of Oceanview's physical inventory observation. Detailed perpetual records would often be available for large, specific identification inventory such as boats.
>
> Note that the auditors counted 100% of the boat inventory, rather than only a sample, because of the significant dollar value of individual boats.

1. Begin by selecting every tenth item from the Inventory Count Sheet (workpapers 22-12 through 22-14), using the top half of workpaper 22-15 to record the boat numbers selected. (Your first stock number should be 8111; your last number should be 8679.)

   Next, trace each of these boat numbers to the Final Inventory Listing (workpapers 22-8 through 22-10) to verify that the boats are listed on the Final Inventory Listing. As you do this, verify that the stock number, manufacturer name, and model number are the same on the count sheet and the inventory listing.

2. Select every tenth item from the Final Inventory Listing (workpapers 22-8 through 22-10), using the bottom half of workpaper 22-15 to record the boat numbers selected. (Your first stock number should be 8009; your last number should be 8778.)

   Next, vouch the boat numbers to the Inventory Count Sheet (workpapers 22-12 through 22-14) to verify that the boats were in the client's possession at year-end (i.e., included in the year-end physical inventory count). As you do this, verify that the stock number, manufacturer name, and model number are the same on the inventory listing and the count sheet.

> **NOTE:** Your testing will be documented on workpaper 22-15. Therefore, it is unnecessary to also document your testing on either the Final Inventory Listing or Inventory Count Sheet.

d. Perform audit program procedure 33 on workpaper 22-6.

To help you perform this step, Bill Cullen has chosen a systematic sample of 30 items on workpapers 22-16 and 22-17.

Assume that, for each of the 30 items selected for testing on workpaper 22-17, Bill compared the price listed on the client's Final Inventory Listing with recent vendors' invoices. Bill found no differences with the exception of three inventory items. Information on the nature of the differences is explained in tickmarks *a*, *b*, and *c* on workpaper 22-10. The invoices for these three items are the last three items in the *Client Documents* booklet.

After reviewing the invoices and reading Bill's notes on workpaper 22-10, complete the six columns in the top section of workpaper 22-18 for the exceptions noted.

> **TIP:** When calculating the "Net misstatement in sample" on workpaper 22-18, overstatements should be treated as positive numbers and understatements as negative numbers.

e.   Complete workpapers 22-18 and 22-19 using the following steps:

> **ELECTRONIC WORKPAPER OPTION:** Complete and print workpaper 22-18 using Excel.
>
> Follow these steps.
>
> 1. Study the numbers and formulas used by Bill on workpaper 22-18 to determine the projected misstatement and the allowance for sampling risk. Make any necessary corrections.
>
> Go to step 3 below.

1.   Calculate the projected misstatement using the formula provided on workpaper 22-18. "Population size (in $)" is the *boat* inventory total from workpaper 22-10. "Sample size (in $)" is the sample total from workpaper 22-17. Round projected misstatement to the nearest dollar.

2.   Assuming the tolerable misstatement is $50,000 for both over- and understatements, use the bottom of workpaper 22-18 to calculate the allowance for sampling risk.

3.   Using your professional judgment, decide whether to:
- accept the population as fairly stated,
- request the client to adjust the account,
- expand your audit tests of inventory, or
- request the client re-work the account.

Re-read step 5 of the sampling steps in Assignment 7 for clarification of this process. Use workpaper 22-19 to document and justify your decision.

f.   On workpaper 22-19, write your conclusion regarding whether inventory is fairly stated or whether further testing will be necessary based on the results of your tests.

g.   Carry forward to workpaper 90-1 your actual and projected misstatement amounts from workpaper 22-18.

> **TIP:** Write the net total actual misstatement in the Identified Misstatement column and the projected misstatement in the Likely Aggregate Misstatement, Current Assets, and Income Before Taxes columns on workpaper 90-1.

Cross-reference the two workpapers by writing *22-18* in the "W/P ref." column on workpaper 90-1, and *90-1* below or to the right of the net sample misstatement and the projected misstatement on workpaper 22-18.

NOTE: In step (g), the assumption is made that the client has, for now, chosen *not* to record an adjusting journal entry to correct the actual misstatements found in your tests. Thus, workpaper 22-2 will be left blank. The Net Adjustments column on workpaper 22-1 will show "0" for each inventory category.

If the client had chosen to correct the misstatements, you would document the adjusting journal entry on workpaper 22-2 and write the net effect of the entry in the Net Adjustments column on workpaper 22-1. In addition, you would enter "0" in the Identified Misstatement column on workpaper 90-1. Your remaining unadjusted projected misstatement would be entered in the Likely Aggregate Misstatement, Current Assets, and Income Before Taxes columns on workpaper 90-1.

Unadjusted actual and projected misstatements are carried forward to the *Summary of Uncorrected Misstatements* (workpaper 90-1). Since the client is not correcting the misstatements at this time, then the actual and projected misstatements you discovered in your tests of inventory are carried forward to the *Summary of Uncorrected Misstatements*. The net amount of the actual misstatements is entered in the Identified Misstatement column, and the net projected misstatement is entered in the Likely Aggregate Misstatement, Current Assets, and Income Before Taxes columns.

h.   Complete step 38 on workpaper 22-7.

i.   On workpaper 22-1, complete the Net Adjustments column by entering "0" for each inventory category. Also complete the 2018 Adjusted Balance column for each inventory category.

Completing the Assignment

Make sure you **signed off** on the following workpapers completed in this assignment, using 2/25/2019 as the date: 22-1, 22-6, 22-7, 22-15, 22-18, and 22-19.

Also make sure you **signed off** on steps 32 and 33 on workpaper 22-6 by writing your initials in the INIT column, added references to appropriate workpapers in the W/P column, and added any appropriate comments in the COMMENTS column.

Group the following items together in the order listed and submit them to your instructor for grading, either in person or online at armonddaltonresources.com (consult your instructor):

- Cover page with your printed name, your signature, and the assignment number.

- Workpapers 22-1, 22-6, 22-7, 22-15, 22-18, and 22-19.

- Answers to discussion questions 1 through 6 (see following four pages) if required by your instructor.

Discussion questions

1. Oceanview's inventory consists primarily of boats and involves a comparatively small number of inventory items. How would inventory observation and test count tracing tests differ if the client has a large number of inventory items and the client did not have a detailed list of inventory on hand at the time of the inventory observation?

    _____

    _____

    _____

    _____

    _____

    _____

    _____

    _____

    _____

    _____

2. Because of the nature of Oceanview's inventory, pricing is done using the specific identification method. How would the pricing tests differ if the inventory consisted of a large number of items for each product?

    _____

    _____

    _____

    _____

    _____

    _____

    _____

    _____

    _____

    _____

    _____

3. Oceanview identified some potentially obsolete inventory items. What tests should the auditor perform to identify inventory that is obsolete or inventory that should be reduced from historical cost to net realizable value?

_____

_____

_____

_____

_____

_____

_____

_____

_____

4. The client received a large shipment of inventory on December 31 during the inventory observation. What procedures should the auditor perform to verify that the acquisition of inventory is properly accounted for?

_____

_____

_____

_____

_____

_____

_____

_____

_____

5. Suppose, while performing analytical procedures, you discover uncollectible sales of *repair parts* have increased significantly from previous years. Although this increase could be due to several factors, explain why this might indicate that one or more employees are stealing *repair parts* from Oceanview.

_____

_____

_____

_____

_____

_____

_____

_____

_____

_____

6. In addition to boats, Oceanview Marine Company's inventory consists of repair parts and supplies, which are susceptible to theft by employees and customers. Describe some internal controls that Oceanview Marine Company should use to prevent and/or detect theft of repair parts and supplies.

_____

_____

_____

_____

_____

_____

_____

_____

_____

Assignment 10: Complete the Audit

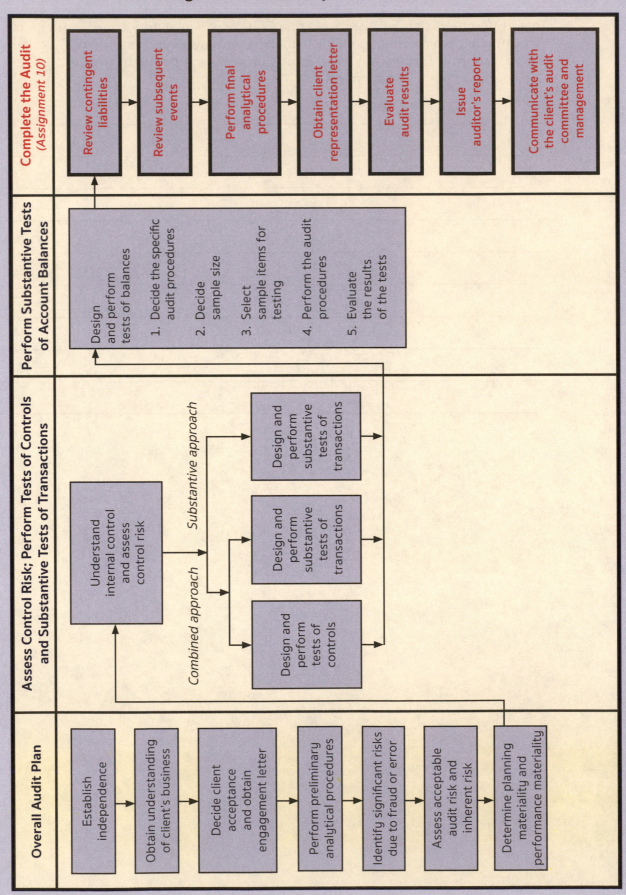

Complete the Audit *(Assignment 10)*

- Review contingent liabilities
- Review subsequent events
- Perform final analytical procedures
- Obtain client representation letter
- Evaluate audit results
- Issue auditor's report
- Communicate with the client's audit committee and management

Perform Substantive Tests of Account Balances

Design and perform tests of balances

1. Decide the specific audit procedures
2. Decide sample size
3. Select sample items for testing
4. Perform the audit procedures
5. Evaluate the results of the tests

Assess Control Risk; Perform Tests of Controls and Substantive Tests of Transactions

Understand internal control and assess control risk

Substantive approach — Design and perform substantive tests of transactions

Combined approach — Design and perform tests of controls → Design and perform substantive tests of transactions

Overall Audit Plan

- Establish independence
- Obtain understanding of client's business
- Decide client acceptance and obtain engagement letter
- Perform preliminary analytical procedures
- Identify significant risks due to fraud or error
- Assess acceptable audit risk and inherent risk
- Determine planning materiality and performance materiality

ASSIGNMENT 10: Complete the Audit

Overview

In this assignment you will:

- ⚓ study the final phase of the audit process.
- ⚓ perform audit procedures involved in completing the Oceanview Marine Company audit engagement.

Auditing concepts

Seven steps to completing the audit

After the auditor completes detailed testing of account balances, he or she must summarize the results of the testing and perform certain general audit procedures before completing the audit engagement. Completing the audit includes the following seven steps:

1. Review contingent liabilities.
2. Review subsequent events.
3. Perform final analytical procedures.
4. Obtain the management representation letter.
5. Evaluate results and determine the sufficiency of audit evidence.
6. Post final adjusting journal entries, prepare financial statements (or assess overall financial statement presentation), and issue the auditor's report.
7. Communicate with the client's audit committee and management.

Each of these seven steps is briefly explained below.

1. **Review contingent liabilities**

   A contingent liability is a potential future obligation to an outside party for an unknown amount that results from events occurring before the balance sheet date. The most common type of contingent liability is a lawsuit that has been filed but not yet resolved. The outcome of a contingent liability is determined by a future event or events. Generally accepted accounting principles specify three levels of probability that a future payment will be made:

   accrued • probable—the chance of the occurrence of the future event(s) is high;
   disclosed • reasonably possible—the chance of the occurrence of the future event(s) is more than remote, but less than probable;
   no action • remote—the chance of the occurrence of the future event(s) is slight.

   The auditor must use professional judgment in analyzing contingent liabilities. If a potential loss is *probable* and the amount can be reasonably estimated, the loss should be accrued as of the balance sheet date. If the potential loss is probable but cannot be reasonably estimated, or if the potential loss is *reasonably possible*, the loss should be disclosed in the notes to the financial statements but not accrued. If the likelihood of potential loss is *remote*, neither accrual nor disclosure is required.

One of the most important audit procedures when reviewing contingent liabilities is to obtain and review letters from the client's attorney(s). Each letter should include a discussion of all pending or threatened litigation handled by the attorney. If an outstanding lawsuit is a contingent liability, the auditor should also obtain the professional opinion of the client's attorney on the expected outcome of the lawsuit and the likely amount of the liability, including court costs.

Other audit procedures that may indicate the existence of contingent liabilities include, but are not limited, to:

- inquiring of management as to the existence of contingent liabilities.
- reviewing minutes of board of directors' meetings for the year.
- reviewing legal invoices supporting legal expense for the year.
- reviewing bank confirmations for the existence of discounted notes receivable or loan guarantees.

2. Review subsequent events

The auditor is required to review certain transactions and events occurring during the period between the balance sheet date and the date of the audit report. There are two types of subsequent events: (1) those that directly affect the financial statements because they provide additional information as to the valuation of an account as of the balance sheet date and (2) significant conditions that did not exist as of the balance sheet date and have no direct effect on the financial statements. The first type of subsequent event, if material, requires adjustment to the financial statements. The second type of subsequent event does not require an adjustment, but disclosure in the financial statement footnotes may be required.

Typical audit procedures performed during subsequent events testing include:

- Review the subsequent year's interim financial statements prepared by the client through the date of the audit report.
- Review the client's general ledger and journals through the date of the audit report.
- Discuss with management events occurring after the balance sheet date but before the date of the audit report. Discussion items may include but are not limited to sales and profit trends; changes in inventory prices or sales prices; purchases of major capital items; initiation of new lawsuits; assessments of federal, state, or local taxes; losses of important customers; related-party transactions; changes in accounting or financial policies; and dividend payments.
- Review minutes of board of directors' meetings held after the year-end.
- Request that the client include a discussion of subsequent events in the representation letter.

> **NOTE:** For this practice case, you can assume that no subsequent events require any adjustments to the financial statements or disclosure.

3. **Perform final analytical procedures**

As explained in Assignment 2, auditing standards require the use of analytical procedures in the audit completion stage of every audit, as well as in the planning stage. In the audit completion stage, analytical procedures provide an overall review of the financial information and assist in the evaluation of the appropriateness of the audit conclusions reached. Analytical procedures performed during the completion stage are an inexpensive final test for material misstatements.

4. **Obtain the management representation letter**

Auditing standards require the auditor to obtain a letter of representation from the client's management. The management representation letter documents management's oral representations made during the audit. The letter is prepared on the client's letterhead and is typically signed by the chief executive officer and chief financial officer.

Although the management representation letter cannot be regarded as reliable evidence due to its nonindependent source, the letter is still useful to the auditor. The letter provides written documentation of responses to management inquiries, should there be a legal dispute between the auditor and the client. Preparation of the representation letter also increases the likelihood that management will better understand its responsibility for the assertions in the financial statements.

5. **Evaluate results and determine the sufficiency of audit evidence**

After completing the specific audit procedures in each audit area, the auditor must evaluate whether sufficient evidence has been accumulated to justify the conclusion that the overall financial statements are fairly stated in accordance with GAAP (or other applicable accounting framework). The first step is to review the audit program and results of each audit area to determine whether the audit objectives have been met. Another important step is to summarize the misstatements discovered in each audit area. Material misstatements should be corrected by the client. Misstatements from each audit area that are not individually material should be summarized so that the combined effect of these misstatements can be compared to the auditor's computed materiality. A convenient workpaper for summarizing these misstatements is the *Summary of Uncorrected Misstatements* (workpaper 90-1).

Two other steps in evaluating the sufficiency of evidence are deciding whether the evidence supports the auditor's opinion and deciding the adequacy of the client's financial statement disclosures. Many CPA firms use a standard financial statement disclosure checklist to assist auditors in this process.

A final step in evidence accumulation and evaluation is the review of the audit workpapers. Proper review helps the firm to be sure that the audit was performed and documented in accordance with professional and firm standards. It also helps the firm evaluate the performance of its audit staff.

6. **Post final adjusting journal entries, prepare financial statements, and issue the auditor's report**

   After completing each audit area and analyzing the *Summary of Uncorrected Misstatements* (workpaper 90-1), the auditor reviews all final adjusting journal entries with the client and posts them to the trial balance. After the entries are posted, the client prepares the financial statements, often with assistance by the auditor. The auditor reviews the financial statements and reconciles them to the leadsheets and trial balance. The auditor should assess the overall financial statement presentation, and then issue the auditor's report.

7. **Communicate with the audit committee and management**

   The auditor is required to communicate certain matters to those charged with governance of the client, such as an audit committee. These matters include:

   - The auditor's responsibility under auditing standards
   - Significant accounting policies
   - Significant audit adjustments
   - Other information in documents containing audited financial statements
   - Disagreements with management
   - Consultation with other accountants
   - Major issues discussed with management prior to retention
   - Difficulties encountered in performing the audit

   Auditing standards require that the auditor communicate all illegal acts and fraud to the client's audit committee or other group charged with governance. The auditor is also required to communicate all significant deficiencies and material weaknesses in internal control identified in the audit to those charged with governance.

   In addition to the required communications described previously, the auditor usually accumulates several suggestions for improving the client's accounting system or business operations. Although not required, the auditor usually includes these items in a management letter. The management letter often promotes good relations between the client and the CPA firm and gives the CPA firm the opportunity to inform the client of additional tax and management advisory services offered by the firm.

Requirements

a. Bill Cullen has completed the subsequent events testing for the Oceanview engagement up to the audit report date, which was the completion of significant audit testing (February 26, 2019).

He documented his work on the subsequent events audit program on workpapers 91-1 and 91-2. Study each step Bill performed on these workpapers to familiarize yourself with the types of audit procedures performed near the end of an audit.

b. Read the management representation letter on workpapers 92-1 through 92-3. Verify that the date of the letter is the same date the audit was completed (February 26, 2019) and has been signed by Oceanview Marine Company's chief executive officer and chief financial officer.

c. Complete the last three columns of the working trial balance (workpapers 3-1 through 3-3).

ELECTRONIC WORKPAPER OPTION: Complete and print workpapers 3-1, 3-2, and 3-3 using Excel. **These workpapers are included in the file named "Assign 2 and 10 Excel_7ed. xlsx."** You may disregard the copies of these workpapers in the *Current Workpapers*.

Follow these steps:

1. Assuming the client has recorded each of the proposed adjusting journal entries shown on workpapers 21-2 and 30-2, complete the "adjustments" column on the trial balance. (Although net income before taxes has changed because of the adjusting journal entries, assume no adjustments to Income Tax Expense are needed.)

2. For each account adjusted in step 1 above, verify that the amount shown in the Income Statement or Balance Sheet column is correct. Make corrections if necessary. (You may need to "unprotect" the worksheet before making corrections by clicking REVIEW, UNPROTECT SHEET.)

3. For the last three rows on the trial balance, verify that the formulas used by Bill to calculate total debits, total credits, and net income are correct. Make corrections if necessary.

4. Verify that the account balances on the financial statements and notes (workpapers 1-1 through 1-5) have been updated correctly to reflect the changes made in the trial balance. Make corrections if necessary.

5. Initial and date (2/26/2019) the working trial balance, the financial statements, and the notes to financial statements.

6. Print the working trial balance, the financial statements, and the notes to financial statements.

---

1. Assuming the client has recorded each of the proposed adjusting journal entries shown on workpapers 21-2 and 30-2, begin by completing the "adjustments" column on the trial balance.
2. Next, complete the balance sheet column by transferring the balances shown in column three for each balance sheet account, after any adjustments.
3. Complete the income statement column by transferring the balances shown in column three for each income statement account, after any adjustments. (Although net income before taxes has changed because of the adjusting journal entries, assume no adjustments to Income Tax Expense are needed.)
4. Complete the last three rows by calculating total debits (adjusted), total credits (adjusted), and net income (adjusted).
5. Update the account balances on the financial statements and notes as needed (workpapers 1-1 through 1-5).
6. Initial and date (2/26/2019) the working trial balance, the financial statements, and the notes to financial statements.

d. On workpaper 90-1 (*Summary of Uncorrected Misstatements*) are several uncorrected misstatements that have been identified during Oceanview's audit. Review and complete the various columns on this sheet by following the steps below:

1. Row a: Total each column by adding the overstatements and subtracting the understatements.

   Row b: Enter, in each column, the measurement base used on workpaper 5-2-a, after adjustments.

   Row c: Enter, in each column, the percentage used on workpaper 5-2-a.

   Row d: Compute materiality by multiplying the adjusted measurement base (row b) and the percentage (row c), rounding your materiality level to the nearest $5,000.

   Row e: For each column, compute the amount remaining for further misstatements by subtracting the *absolute value* of the column total (row a) from materiality (row d). (The amount remaining for further uncorrected misstatements is similar in concept to an "allowance for sampling risk.")

2. In the conclusion section on the bottom of workpaper 90-1, state your opinion whether the amount remaining for further uncorrected misstatements is adequate. (Assume no other unadjusted differences were found in the other sections of the audit.)

e. Write an appropriate auditor's report. Date and sign the report, using your firm's name. (The audit was completed on February 26, 2019.)

NOTE: Although Oceanview is issuing comparative financial statements for three years (2018, 2017, and 2016), your audit report should express an opinion only on the 2018 financial statements. The 2017 and 2016 financial statements were audited by a different CPA firm – Talbert & Johnson, CPAs. At the request of Oceanview's management, Talbert & Johnson has agreed to reissue its audit reports for 2017 and 2016, both of which expressed unmodified opinions. These reports were dated March 29, 2018, and March 15, 2017, respectively.

f.   Add one additional recommendation to the management letter items (workpapers 93-1 and 93-2, which you turned in for grading previously) based on your work in Assignments 1 through 10. Initial and date workpapers 93-1 and 93-2, using 2/26/2019 as the date.

Completing the Assignment

Group the following items together in the order listed and submit them to your instructor for grading, either in person or online at armonddaltonresources.com (consult your instructor):

- Cover page with your printed name, your signature, and the assignment number.
- Workpapers 1-1 through 1-5, 3-1 through 3-3, 90-1, 93-2, and your auditor's report.
- Answer to discussion questions 1 through 4 (see next two pages) if required by your instructor.

Discussion questions

1. What period is covered by the auditor's review for subsequent events? Give an example of a subsequent event that should result in **disclosure**, and a subsequent event that would require **adjustment** to the financial statements.

_____

_____

_____

_____

_____

_____

2. Assume you learn of a subsequent event after the date of the audit report (end of audit fieldwork) but before the audit report has been issued. How should you address this type of subsequent event?

_____

_____

_____

_____

_____

_____

3. Your preliminary judgment of materiality was based on net income. Why is it necessary to compare unadjusted misstatements to other bases of materiality? What should the auditor do if the unadjusted misstatements exceed one or more materiality thresholds?

_____

_____

_____

_____

_____

_____

4. Why must the auditor review and obtain the client's approval of adjusting journal entries before posting them to the trial balance? What should the auditor do if the client does not agree with the proposed adjustments?

_____

_____

_____

_____

_____

_____

This Page Intentionally Blank

PERMANENT FILE

> **Note:** A permanent file contains information of a permanent, on-going nature about the client as shown in the permanent file index below. In this practice case, only the workpapers in section 100 (Audit Planning) of the permanent file have been included. The rest of the workpapers in the permanent file are not needed for this practice case and have not been included.

Permanent File Index

Section 100—Audit Planning:

- (101) Client background information
- (102) Chart of accounts
- (103) Client acceptance form
- (104) Organization chart
- (105) Appointment of auditor letter
- (106) Audit takeover letter and reply
- (107) Shareholder resolutions

Section 200—Articles of Incorporation and Contracts:

- 201 Articles of incorporation and partnership agreements
- 202 Amendments to articles and agreements
- 203 Bylaws
- 204 Minutes — directors, shareholders, executive, partners, members
- 205 Mortgages
- 206 Leases
- 207 Bond indemnities
- 208 Pension plans, profit sharing plans
- 209 Executive compensation agreements (including stock options)
- 210 Union or other employee agreements

Section 300—Carryforward Schedules:

- 301 Long-term assets
- 302 Long-term debt
- 303 Stock, additional paid-in capital, retained earnings

Client background information

History of Oceanview Marine Company

Oceanview Marine Company (Oceanview) operates a marina and is the largest dealer of new and used boats in Ocean City, Florida. Oceanview's products include new and used powerboats and sailboats, repair parts for boats, and general marine supplies. Boats sold by Oceanview range in price from more than $200,000 for 40-foot cabin cruisers to less than $2,000 for small sailboats. Parts include a variety of replacement items for motors, boats, sails, and related equipment. Marine supplies include hundreds of items of interest to marine enthusiasts including clothing, water-ski equipment, suntan lotions, and fishing equipment. Oceanview rents a warehouse to keep its boats and parts inventory.

In addition to products, Oceanview provides several services and rents smaller powerboats, sailboats, and paddleboats. Repair services are available for motors, boats, and equipment. Oceanview also has dock space available for monthly or daily rental, as well as launching ramps for boats.

A major reason for Oceanview's success has been the way customers are treated, including a unique credit policy. Customers who purchase a boat of any size from Oceanview are granted credit for that purchase and for any services and products. There is no interest charged on accounts receivable, unless the receivable is more than $500 and more than 90 days outstanding. In effect, a customer can buy a boat interest-free for the first three months. After three months, interest rates are 2% above the prime rate. It is not uncommon for regular customers to come off the water and order food and beverages and "put it on the tab." Oceanview also accepts checks of up to $2,500 from customers without obtaining a credit check.

These liberal credit policies have resulted in extraordinary customer loyalty; customers often get a feeling of belonging to a marine club without a membership fee. **Donald Phillips, the company president,** knows most of the customers, their spouses, and their children by name and operates the business in a friendly, customer satisfaction-oriented manner. He works hard to minimize employee turnover. Most employees also know customers by name and treat them with extreme courtesy.

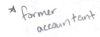 * former accountant

Roger T. Phillips started the company in 1961 under the name of Phillips Boats and Minnows. The company operated as a sideline for Roger, who was semi-retired and an avid fisherman. Upon Roger's death in 1990, his grandson, Donald, inherited Phillips Boats and Minnows. Don graduated from Florida State University in 1983 with an accounting degree and was working for a CPA firm in Jacksonville at the time of his grandfather's death. Shortly thereafter, Don decided to leave the CPA firm to go into the marine business. He immediately incorporated the business and changed the name of the business to Oceanview Marine Company. Under Don's entrepreneurship, the company grew rapidly and successfully. In 2008, the company's rapid growth created a severe cash shortage. Don decided to finance the growth by selling 30% of the business to an outside investor group, **Southeastern Enterprises** (Southeastern), for $300,000. Southeastern also made a long-term loan of $564,200 to Oceanview at an interest rate equal to the bank prime rate. The interest is calculated and paid monthly. In addition to interest, the principal is repayable at $5,642 per year, with a final balloon payment of the remaining loan balance due in the year 2020. The agreement permits Southeastern to have two members on the Board of Directors. The current members from Southeastern are Nathan Andrews and Elva Schmidt. Don considers the Southeastern members cooperative in managing the business; however, they object if officers' salaries or fringe benefits are excessive. Oceanview Marine Company pays annual dividends to provide a return on Southeastern Enterprise's investment. Don has been in negotiations to buy-out Southeastern's interest, but they have not been able to agree on terms. In retrospect, Don wishes he had not used outside investors' money to finance Oceanview's growth.

Privately held company

Don also arranged with the bank for a revolving line of credit secured by accounts receivable and inventory. The interest rate has been set at bank prime rate plus 1%. Interest is calculated on the daily balance and charged to the account once a month. The bank reviews the line of credit annually, usually after the audit. For 2018, the credit limit was set to 40% of the audited book value of inventory and net accounts receivable at December 31, 2017.

Arvin Phillips, Don's son, joined the company in 2008 after finishing his education in marketing at his father's alma mater. **Cynthia Rathberg**, Don's daughter, joined the firm in 2014 as controller. Cynthia graduated in accounting from Michigan State University in 2008 and spent three years with a national CPA firm in Atlanta. Both Arvin and Cynthia are involved very closely in the business operations and are familiar with the computer systems and software used in the business. During the past three years, Don has gradually transferred some ownership of the business and management responsibilities to the two children. Don currently holds 50% of the shares, and Arvin and Cynthia each own 10% of the shares.

History of the Audit

In 2006, after the Internal Revenue Service assessed the company $28,000 for underpayment of taxes and penalties, Don decided he wanted a CPA firm to prepare the company's tax returns. Don engaged the Tampa CPA firm of **Talbert and Johnson, PC**. In 2008, Southeastern required an independent audit as part of the investment agreement. Oceanview hired Talbert and Johnson to do the audit.

On several occasions during the past three years, Cynthia expressed to her father the belief that a CPA firm in the local community would be more accessible and provide better services at the same or lower cost. Her father agreed to change auditors for the current year's audit (December 31, 2018). After receiving bids and interviewing the three largest CPA firms in Ocean City, Don and Cynthia selected our firm, **Lilts Berger & Associates, CPAs**.

In early October 2018, the engagement partner, **Charles Ward**, did an extensive investigation of Oceanview before accepting the engagement. The most important part of the investigation was to talk with Bob Talbert of Talbert and Johnson to investigate his firm's relationship with, and attitudes about, Oceanview and its employees. Bob Talbert was complimentary about Oceanview and spoke highly of its employees' integrity, competence, and dedication to running a successful business. Mr. Talbert understood the reason for the change in auditors and was not surprised. He offered to provide our firm access to the prior years' workpapers if Oceanview granted written permission and Talbert and Johnson was paid for any time spent. Oceanview authorized our firm to review the prior years' workpapers and compensated Talbert and Johnson accordingly.

Mr. Ward contacted Oceanview's banker and attorney and several local suppliers who do business with Oceanview. He also examined Oceanview's 2016 and 2017 audited financial statements and calculated several financial ratios. Based upon all of the information he obtained, Mr. Ward concluded that Oceanview would be an excellent client. He completed the CLIENT ACCEPTANCE FORM and AUDIT TAKE-OVER LETTER (see workpapers 103-1 to 103-8 and 106-1 in the permanent file). He also prepared an ENGAGEMENT LETTER outlining the terms of the audit engagement. Don Phillips signed the engagement letter indicating his agreement with those terms. The engagement letter is in the current workpaper file, workpapers 4-1 through 4-3.

Significant Accounting Policies—
Oceanview Marine Company

1.   Allowance for doubtful accounts

Oceanview Marine Company computes an allowance for doubtful accounts based on the amount and age of receivables outstanding.

The allowance for doubtful accounts is based on:
Current receivables	3% of balance
Outstanding 31 to 60 days	10% of balance
Outstanding 61 to 90 days	15% of balance
Over 90 days	30% of balance

2.   Inventories

Inventories are recorded at the lower of cost or market using specific identification for boats and FIFO for all other inventories to determine cost of goods sold and cost of ending inventory. Perpetual inventory accounting procedures are followed.

3.   Fixed Assets

a.   **Trade-ins:** The company's policy is not to record a gain or loss on disposal of similar (like-kind) property.

b.   **Depreciation:** Automobiles and equipment are depreciated at 30% and 20% respectively using the declining balance method. Other fixed assets are depreciated using the straight-line method. The company's policy is to record a half-year of depreciation in the year of acquisition and disposal.

4.   Pension Plan

The company has a defined contribution pension plan for employees who qualify. The company keeps the contributions current, and there is no difference between the value of the pension assets and the value of the pension plan liabilities at each year-end.

Accounting Records

In early 2015, Cynthia recommended that the company implement a computerized, networked accounting system based on Sage 50 accounting software and six personal computers running on a Windows network. The Board of Directors approved the acquisition in May, and the company purchased the equipment and software on June 15, 2015. Cynthia spent the remainder of the year experimenting with the system, including running the new computer system and the old manual system simultaneously. The company converted to the computerized system on January 1, 2016. The following records are on the accounting system:

Records

Cash receipts journal
Cash disbursements journal
Sales journal
Payroll journal and related records
General ledger
Subsidiary records:
  Accounts receivable
  Accounts payable
  Perpetual inventory

The Sage 50 accounting system generates comparative financial statements on the company's networked printer. Cynthia examines this data in detail and discusses it with Don if there are any significant changes or indications of business problems. Cynthia also has the system generate monthly listings of accounts receivable and accounts payable, a trial balance, and a perpetual inventory listing in terms of quantities and dollars. Cynthia uses a backup system to ensure that no disruption of service would arise during a system failure.

Chart of Accounts

Account	Description
1010	Petty cash
1015	Bank — payroll
1020	Bank — general
1100	Accounts receivable
1110	Allowance for doubtful accounts
1205	Inventory — boats
1210	Inventory — repair parts
1215	Inventory — supplies
1300	Prepaid expenses
1400	Deposits
1500	Land
1510	Automobiles
1511	Accum. depreciation — automobiles
1520	Equipment
1521	Accum. depreciation — equipment
1530	Office equipment
1531	Accum. depreciation — office equip.
1540	Building
1541	Accum. depreciation — building
1550	Docks
1551	Accum. depreciation — docks
2010	Accounts payable — trade
2100	Wages and salaries payable
2110	Payroll withholdings payable
2200	Federal income taxes payable
2300	Interest payable
2400	Notes payable — bank
2500	Long-term debt — current portion
2710	Long-term debt
3100	Common stock
3200	Additional paid-in capital
3500	Retained earnings
3510	Dividends paid
4100	Sales revenue
4500	Sales returns and allowances
5100	Cost of goods sold
6010	Accounting fees
6020	Advertising
6050	Depreciation
6100	Bad debt expense
6120	Business publications
6240	Cleaning service
6530	Fuel

Chart of Accounts

Account	Description
6810	Garbage collection
6820	Insurance
6830	Interest
7110	Legal
7130	Licensing & certification fees
7150	Linen service
7230	Miscellaneous
7420	Office supplies
7560	Postage
7580	Property taxes
7620	Rent — warehouse
7630	Repairs and maintenance
7710	Security
7810	Telephone
7850	Travel and entertainment
7980	Utilities
9100	Salaries — management
9110	Salaries — office
9120	Salaries — sales
9200	Wages — mechanics
9210	Wages — rental
9220	Wages — warehouse
9500	Payroll benefits
9600	Medical benefits
9610	Pension expense
9900	Income tax expense

Totals: 67 Accounts

Client Acceptance Form

INSTRUCTIONS: This form should be prepared by the in-charge senior, engagement manager, or engagement partner for all new clients. The engagement partner and the office managing partner should review the data as a basis for initially accepting or rejecting the client. The in-charge senior and engagement manager should update and review the form annually during the pre-engagement planning as a basis for maintaining a basic understanding of the client and for retaining or terminating the client. This form should be reviewed annually by the engagement partner and the office managing partner before the engagement begins.

Part I — Basic Client Information

1. Legal Name *Oceanview Marine Company*   Phone *555-2522*

    Legal Address *36 Clearwater Lake Road*   FAX *555-2523*

    Ocean City, Florida   ZIP Code *33140*

    Year-end *December 31, 2018*

    Primary Contact *Cynthia Rathberg (controller)*   Phone *555-2522*

2. Organization:

    _____ Corporation — publicly-held

    ___✓___ Corporation — non-public

    _____ Partnership

    _____ Association/Society

    _____ Trust

    _____ Other

    Date and Location of Formation: *Incorporated June 6, 1990 in Ocean City, Florida*

3. Significant Shareholders/Partners:

Name	Position	Shareholdings	Relationship
Donald C. Phillips	*President*	*50% voting shares*	*Father*
Arvin Phillips	*Vice Pres.*	*10% voting shares*	*Son*
Cynthia Rathberg	*Controller*	*10% voting shares*	*Daughter*
Southeastern Enterprises	*2 members of board of directors*	*30% voting shares*	*Outside Investor*

4. Officers and Directors:

Name	Position
Donald C. Phillips	President
Arvin Phillips	Vice-president

5. Related Companies:

Name	Relationship
Deep Sea Charter	50% owned by Donald Phillips

Note: Deep Sea Charter is a charter business that, in the past, has bought their boats from Oceanview Marine Company. However, there have been no material transactions between the two companies during the past 5 years.

6. Client's Lawyer:

Name
Frederickson, Marcus & Lane

Address
3611 Pine Avenue
Ocean City, Florida 33142

7. Client's Financial Institution:

Name
First National Bank of Ocean City

Address
317 Fifth Avenue
Ocean City, Florida 33140

8. Client's Transfer Agent (if applicable):

Name
N/A — privately-held company

Address

9. Client's Insurance Agent:

Name
Hanson & Row

Address
14 North Main Street
Ocean City, Florida 33142

10. Describe the client's business.

    Retail sales of boats, supplies, repair service and parts, and boat rentals. Current business has existed for more than 50 years. Assets of $17 million and sales of $26 million.

11. List the location, purpose and number of employees of all business premises (office, plants, and warehouses).

    Company is at only one location: 36 Clearwater Lake Road, Ocean City, Florida.
    See organization chart for details regarding employees (W/P 104).

12. List major sources of revenue and major customers (include percentage of revenue).

    Local boat owners —— no major customers; company has numerous accounts.

13. List major suppliers and nature of supply.

    No major suppliers; company has numerous suppliers.

14. List major sources of financing (loans, leases).

Line of credit with First National Bank of Ocean City.

Loan agreement with shareholder — Southeastern Enterprises

15. Describe compensation and employee benefit plans.

Regular salary and wages plus an additional bonus paid in December or January of the

following year — determined by Donald Phillips. If not paid in December, it is accrued to avoid

manipulation of net income.

16. Does the client's industry adhere to any specialized accounting practices?

None other than GAAP.

17. Are there any statutes or regulations that may directly affect the client's financial statements?

No

18. Are there any external conditions or trends that may have a significant impact on the client, such as changes in buyers, changes in suppliers, or new competitors? Will these changes impact the client as a going concern?

No

19.   Services to be provided:

Description	Year		
	2018	*2019*	*2020*
Audit of financial statements	✓		
SEC Reporting:			
Annual			
Quarterly reviews			
Registration			
Other			
Accounting:			
Review			
Compilation			
Bookkeeping			
Taxes:			
Return preparation			
Return review	✓		
Consultation:			
Tax planning	✓		
Consulting services			
Other reports and services:			
_____			
_____			

Will the financial statements and audit report be
used for high risk purposes such as SEC filings,
performance bonds, or litigation (yes, no)?

No *

If yes, explain: **company is considering raising additional capital and would consider a public offering within the
next two or three years to finance possible expansion to additional locations.*

Describe how the financial statements and audit report will be used:
*The audit has been an annual requirement of Southeastern Enterprises for 10 years. Also,
management likes to use F/S for management information and control. Finally, the audit is
required under line-of-credit agreement with First National Bank.*

20. Schedule for performance and completion:

Type of Service/Report	Deadline		
	2018	*2019*	*2020*
Begin interim fieldwork	*12-1 (2018)*		
Completion of fieldwork	*3-15 (2019)*		
Delivery of management letter	*3-22 (2019)*		
Delivery of audit report	*3-29 (2019)*		
Delivery of tax returns	*3-29 (2019)*		

21. Billing arrangements:

Audit and tax services fees will be based on hourly rates. Invoices will be submitted to the client periodically as the work progresses. Invoices are payable upon presentation. Total fees are estimated to be $32,000. Client to be notified of any changes in estimated fees.

22. Are there potential going-concern problems with which we should be concerned (yes, no; describe any major concerns on separate sheet)?

Year	Going Concern Problems (yes, no)?	Comments
2018	*No*	*Profitable and solvent*
2019		
2020		

23. Expected client assistance:

Cynthia Rathberg and staff will provide maximum assistance in preparing data and providing documents and records. We should give the client sufficient notice of all required audit schedules and document requests.

24. Are there any financial, employment, or family relationships among our firm's staff or partners and client personnel that would appear to impair our independence (yes, no; if yes, describe)?

No

Part II — Initial Client Acceptance Information

1. Communication with predecessor auditors:

    a. Name and address of predecessor auditors

        Name

        Talbert and Johnson

        Address

        509 North Florida Avenue

        Tampa, Florida 33613

    b. Have the requirements concerning communications with predecessor auditors been met?

        Yes

    c. Reason for changing auditors?

        Cynthia Rathberg, controller, wants to work with a CPA firm in Ocean City.

    d. Are there any fees owed to the prior auditors?

        _No_

    e. Have the prior auditors been consulted? If not, why not?

        Yes. Parting was friendly.

    f. Do you believe the prior auditors will cooperate with us?

        Yes

    g. Can we review the prior auditor's workpapers?

        Yes

2. New Client Data:

a. Firm personnel developing client: _Charles Ward, partner_

b. Source of referral:

<u>Type</u>   <u>Name and Affiliation</u>

   i.   Personal acquaintance
        of firm personnel:

   ii.   By another client:

   iii.   By attorney:

   iv.   By banker:

   v.   Other: _Client — Donald Phillips interviewed several CPA firms in Ocean City._

c. New client investigation procedures:

		Done by:	Date
i.	Contact predecessor CPAs:	_CW_	_10-12-2018_
ii.	Contact client references, e.g., banks, attorneys, others:	_CW_	_10-12-2018_
iii.	Obtain credit report for company and/or principal officers, e.g., D&B, credit bureau:	_CW_	_10-12-2018_
iv.	Review recent financial statements and accountant's reports, tax returns, etc.:	_CW_	_10-12-2018_
v.	Evaluate firm's independence of conflict of interest problems:	_CW_	_10-19-2018_

Prepared by: _Charles Ward_   Date _10-19-2018_
(In-charge senior, manager, or partner)

<u>Client Acceptance:</u>

Approved by: _Charles Ward_   Date _10-19-2018_
(Engagement partner)

Approved by: _Herbert Lilts_   Date _10-19-2018_
(Managing partner)

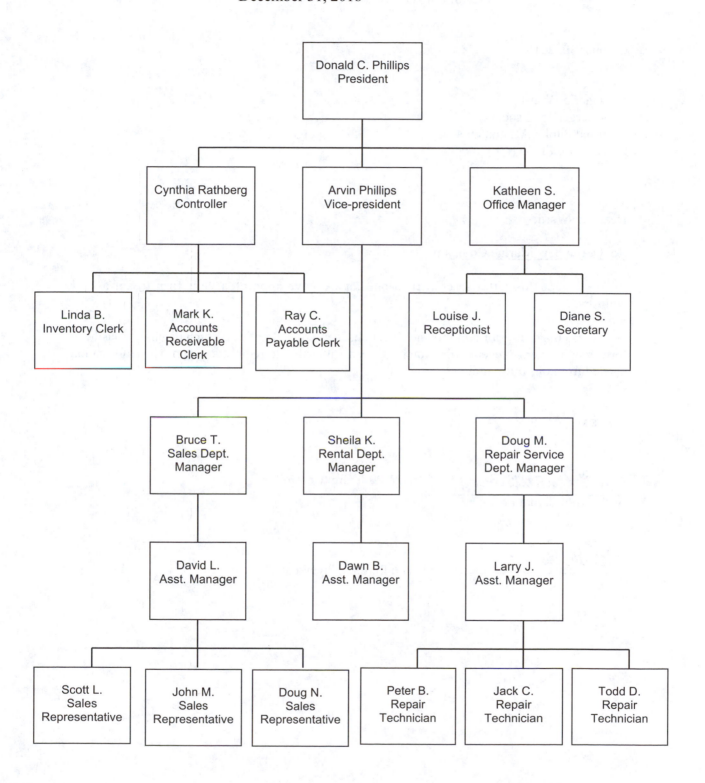

OCEANVIEW MARINE COMPANY
36 Clearwater Lake Road
Ocean City, Florida 33140

October 30, 2018

Mr. Charles Ward
Lilts Berger & Associates
Certified Public Accountants
Ocean City, FL 33140

Dear Mr. Ward:

Re: Oceanview Marine Company

Please accept this letter as confirmation that we have appointed your firm to act as our auditors.

We advise that our prior auditors have been discharged, and notice of such discharge has been forwarded to them. Accordingly, you have been authorized to request any pertinent information needed from our prior auditors.

Yours very truly,

Cynthia Rathberg
_____
Authorized Signature

Cynthia Rathberg, Controller

Donald Phillips
_____
Authorized Signature

Donald Phillips, President

October 30, 2018

Mr. J. Talbert
Talbert and Johnson
Certified Public Accountants
509 North Florida Avenue
Tampa, FL 33613

Dear Mr. Talbert:

Re: Oceanview Marine Company

We have been approached by Oceanview Marine Company, which has requested our firm to act as their auditors. Please advise whether or not there is any reason that may preclude our acceptance of this appointment, or any information of which we should be aware. We would appreciate your response in writing.

Should there be no professional reason that would preclude our acceptance of this appointment, we request that you provide us with a copy of your financial statement workpaper files.

Enclosed is a copy of Oceanview Marine Company's authorization letter.

Sincerely,

Lilts Berger & Associates

Per: *Charles Ward*
_____
Charles Ward, CPA
Partner

TALBERT AND JOHNSON
Certified Public Accountants
Tampa, Florida 33613

November 4, 2018

Mr. Charles Ward
Lilts Berger & Associates
Certified Public Accountants
Ocean City, FL 33140

Dear Mr. Ward:

Re: Oceanview Marine Company

In reply to your letter regarding acceptance of your appointment as the auditors for the above-mentioned company, we know of no professional reason that should preclude your acceptance of this appointment.

Enclosed is a copy of our financial statement workpaper files as requested.

Sincerely,

Talbert and Johnson

___J. Talbert___

J. Talbert, CPA
Partner

Minutes of Meeting of Directors of Oceanview Marine Company. Held at the registered office of the Company, 36 Clearwater Lake Road, Ocean City, Florida 33140, on October 30, 2018.

PRESENT:
    Donald Phillips
    Arvin Phillips
    Cynthia Rathberg
    *Nathan Andrews
    *Elva Schmidt
    (being all the directors of the Company)

    *representing Southeastern Enterprises

Donald Phillips acted as chairman and Arvin Phillips acted as the secretary of the meeting.

All the directors being present and having waived notice of the meeting, the meeting was declared to be regularly constituted.

On the direction of the chairman, the secretary of the meeting read the minutes of the meeting of Directors held on August 28, 2018, which minutes were duly considered and, insofar as the directors are capable were duly approved as read.

Auditor

UPON MOTION duly made and seconded, IT WAS UNANIMOUSLY RESOLVED that the appointment of the current auditor, Talbert and Johnson, Certified Public Accountants, be terminated, and that Lilts Berger & Associates, Certified Public Accountants, be appointed auditors of the company effective immediately, at a remuneration to be fixed by the directors.

There being no further business, the meeting then adjourned.

Donald Phillips
_____
Donald Phillips

Arvin Phillips
_____
Arvin Phillips

NOTES